The Power of Fantasy in Early Learning

'From the story of the fantasy life of this classroom, Jenny Tyrrell builds an even richer tale, which teaches all of us how effective we can be in extending children's imagination, and ultimately in teaching them how to live. There can be no more important role of a teacher.'

Professor Colin Harrison, University of Nottingham

'This is a book that every primary school teacher can read with delight and benefit.'

Kieran Egan, Simon Fraser University, British Columbia

The Power of Fantasy in Early Learning is Jenny Tyrrell's absorbing and thought-provoking account of her success in using fantasy figures to develop literacy in her pupils. This unique book describes an alternative route to learning which harnessed and constantly stimulated the imaginations of young children; a sustained imaginative environment emerged in which learning flourished. Beautifully written by an experienced early years teacher, *The Power of Fantasy in Early Learning* is at the same time a guide to classroom practice, a challenge to conventional literacy techniques and an inspiring story.

Jenny Tyrrell was a primary school teacher for twenty years before becoming a teacher educator. She is the author, with Narinderjit Gill, of *Co-ordinating English at Key Stage One* (RoutledgeFalmer, 2000).

The Power of Fantasy in Early Learning

Jenny Tyrrell

Illustrated by David Schofield

London and New York

First published 2001
by RoutledgeFalmer
11 New Fetter Lane, London EC4P 4EE

Simultaneously published in the USA and Canada
by RoutledgeFalmer
29 West 35th Street, New York, NY 10001

RoutledgeFalmer is an imprint of the Taylor & Francis Group

© 2001 Jenny Tyrrell
Illustrations © David Schofield

Typeset in Sabon by M Rules
Printed and bound in Great Britain by
TJ International Ltd, Padstow, Cornwall

British Library Cataloguing-in-Publication Data
A catalogue record for this book is available from the
British Library

Library of Congress Cataloging-in-Publication Data
Tyrrell, Jenny.
    The power of fantasy in early learning: real on the inside/Jenny Tyrrell.
        p.   cm.
    Includes bibliographical references.
1. Language arts (Primary) – Case studies. 2. Fantasy in children – Case
studies. 3. Interdisciplinary approach in education – Case studies. 4. Early
childhood education – Activity programs – Case studies. I. Title.

LB1528.T97 2001
372.6—dc21   2001019141

ISBN 0 415 24021 2

Tell me where is fancy bred,
Or in the heart or in the head?
Where begot, how nourished?
Reply, Reply.

It is engender'd in the eyes,
With gazing fed; and fancy dies
In the cradle where it lies.
Let us all ring fancy's knell;
I'll begin it, Ding, dong, bell.

William Shakespeare, *The Merchant of Venice*,
Act 3, Scene 2

Contents

Figures

Illustrations

Preface

I am a teacher. Everything I say, everything I do, everything I write, is coloured by my professional beliefs based on who I am, what matters to me and why I think in this way. I believe that the central task of the teacher is to feed the learner's curiosity, to fire and then kindle the imagination, to nurture the self-esteem and to let each learner discover who they are as learners, thus enabling learning to be effective and lasting. I believe that when young children come to school they have a right to enjoy the experience. There should be enough space in our busy schooldays and often over-filled curriculum, for children to have fun, for we learn best at any age those things we enjoy doing. The skill for teachers is to weave this vitally strong thread into the fabric of daily school life in the realisation that it is an essential feature.

I have an overpowering need to tell this story, for this is what it is, the story of an experienced teacher and two groups of uniquely individual children. I write this for anyone who is interested in the way young children assimilate formal learning in institutionalised systems. I hope it will lead the reader to question what we do in the name of education and be open to the suggestion of alternative routes.

Acknowledgements

To all those people who have encouraged me to write this story I say 'thank you' for pushing me. A special 'thank you' to my editor Anna Clarkson for being supportive and encouraging. To my daughter Clare, who had the original idea and who, in the last twelve months, has been my greatest critic and a tireless proof-reader. To David Schofield, many thanks for agreeing to do the illustrations. Also thanks to Robyn Wishart, a young, enthusiastic teacher who kindly agreed to read the finished text and give valuable feedback.

Special thanks go to Maura Coultous, Janet Wiltshire and Linda Speed who were there in school, encouraging and enjoying the experiences with the children.

Finally, to the children who made all this possible, it is dedicated to you all with love. Your names have been changed but I hope you can recognise yourselves if this book comes your way.

Introduction
'Tell me where is fancy bred?'

To me, fantasy and the development of the imagination are an integral part of growing up. As teachers we are often heard to say, 'capture their interest and you are away', but for how long? I believe that I happened upon a way to harness this force to create a sustained imaginative environment in which deep learning flourished.

I have eighteen years teaching experience at primary level. I believe they were productive years for the children and myself. The last two years, however, teaching 6 year olds, were different from the rest. In those years my classroom was a place where fantasy became the main motivational element in the children's learning. In the first year there was a large stuffed bear living in the corner of the classroom and during the second year, a small witch who came out of a storybook and caused havoc in the classroom for a full year.

The children became totally involved with these characters, as did I, as did everybody who came into contact with the children. The atmosphere in the classroom was noticeably different. There was an air of shared enjoyment, genuine happiness and pleasure in learning that I don't think I had ever managed to make a permanent feature throughout a year before. Above all, the children worked consistently, totally absorbed in their learning. The heightened imagination seemed to permeate every aspect of the school day, in particular their literacy acquisition.

In order to contextualise what I am going to write, the reader should be aware of some of the formative influences in my background. 'Fancy' was bred in me in a rather isolated country childhood. I was happy and secure for the first five years and then, one morning I was put on a bus and travelled the ten miles to the nearest town to attend a small school for girls. I don't think that I really knew what school was until it started. I didn't know anyone and there was certainly no gentle transition with brief visits before the real thing began. The journey to and from school seemed interminable. When I was little I used to spend a lot of time imagining whom I would choose to be my parents if the world were to stop for everyone except the occupants of our bus. As I grew older I would wait in excruciating anticipation for the bus driver to negotiate a particular corner. If he hit the curb then I would fail the eleven plus examination and would not be able to go to the grammar school. If he didn't hit it then I would pass.

I was 'taught' by kind, ageless, seemingly genderless nuns, whose qualifications to teach would, I am sure, be questioned today. I have wonderful memories of hot summer days when afternoon lessons were often abandoned and we would go for a 'nature walk'. This title gave educational purpose to a stroll through the gardens, which usually culminated at the lily pond. There we would lie around the edge of the pond, trailing our fingers in the water as we observed the pond life. We then wandered back and pored over books in an attempt to identify what we had seen. I know a great deal about newts, frogs and assorted pond life, the learning of which was deeply absorbed in a relaxed environment, which allowed time to think and questions to form.

At the age of eleven, due no doubt to the bus driver's improved skills at negotiating corners, I moved on to the local grammar school for girls. There I learned facts, which were regurgitated in tests and examinations, long before digestion had taken place. As a result, my self-esteem as a learner went down and down. I was learning in a way that had no foundation in previous knowledge or understanding and can say with certainty that I remember nothing of what I learned there in those seven years of privileged education, other than random facts about Greek and Roman pillars and the climatic conditions that affect wheat growing in the Prairies. I did learn how to pass examinations if that is the purpose of formal education.

I then went on to be 'educated' to become a teacher with a divergent learning background but a focused understanding of the sort of teacher I wanted to be. Somehow I had to bring 'lily pond' learning into my classrooms. In urban schools this was obviously impossible in the literal sense, so I started working on ways to create imaginative environments. I have memories of classrooms transformed into rain forests, deserts and arctic scenes. Of the time we made a huge spider's web, which covered the classroom ceiling and hung paper spiders and flies from the string web. These 'topic-related' extravaganzas were great fun and very motivating, but they were short-lived as they only lasted for the duration of the topic. I remember vividly the 'spider' children begging me to leave the web because they loved to come into their very different class-room, but it was pulled down to make room for something else. In so doing I must have destroyed all of the magic I had created. I also probably slowed down the momentum of the learning of many of the children. At that time I just hadn't realised the full potential of what I was doing. In retrospect I can see that the experiences were a natural progression towards the years with the Bear and the Little Witch that I am now about to recount.

I believe that any teacher, in any educational system, can build on young children's innate enjoyment of make-believe and plan their teaching to utilise this powerful force. Nothing I am about to describe needs more than an ability to say, 'Let's pretend' and the confidence to follow the children's lead within a framework of professional knowledge.

Chapter 1

'Or in the heart or in the head'

Chapter 1

'Or in the heart or in the head'

It was the end of August and I was contemplating the needs of the class I was about to begin working with for a year. They were the youngest class in the year band and although they were to be in primary 2, most of them would not be six until this first term. There was a rather large group of immature boys who had made little visible literacy progress during their first year in school. However, they were bright, alert and articulate and hopefully ready for rapid progress! There was one little girl who was a cause for concern because she had chosen not to speak in the previous class for the two months that she had attended the school. Her only utterances were for essential needs like 'toilet'. Her parents assured us that she spoke at home, but there had been many upheavals and changes during her short life. There was another child with a heart condition that meant she needed particular care and attention. Of the group, six children had English as an additional language.

I really wanted these children to feel the high priority that I give to reading, so I was keen to capture their interest in books straight-away. I found just the text I was looking for in *We're Going on a Bear Hunt* by Michael Rosen and Helen Oxenbury. In this book were all the ingredients I needed. There was a gripping story, an easily remembered repetitive pattern, predictability, suspense, excellent illustrations and it was large enough for all the children to see when I held the book up.

I copied the text onto big sheets of card, using colour to high-light different aspects of the text, in particular the repetitive pattern. I then pinned them up around the room and stood back to admire my handiwork. It was at this point that Bear's conception occurred. My thirteen-year-old daughter had come to school with me because she was bored with the holidays and said that she would come to 'help' me. In retrospect I am pleased that my stress levels were so low that I said 'yes', for such help usually involved valuable time being spent finding things to occupy the helper. She looked at the story around the walls and said, 'You know what we should do, Mum, we should make a Bear, a big Bear and put him in a cave in the corner.' I agreed because it seemed a good way to keep her occupied while I got on with important tasks. Clare went off to the cupboards where all the costumes are kept for assemblies and plays. She came back about half an hour later with a brown woolly bear suit, that would fit an eleven-year-old child, paws, feet and head dress in the same fabric and yards and yards of black fabric which had been bought to be used as a backdrop. The only material that we had to hand to stuff the suit was newspaper. Bear was stuffed with screwed-up paper and so he took shape, albeit rather a lumpy shape. We had a problem with the head as obviously a child's angelic face was supposed to smile from the headpiece. This problem was solved by using a pair of brown tights, stuffed with newspaper. The legs went into the body and the 'bottom' made a chubby head. By this stage we were getting enthusiastic and so the eyes were cut out from felt and carefully stitched into place along with a nose and smiling mouth. The black fabric was draped in one corner and Bear was put inside his cave. To accompany him there was a jam jar, bearing a label decorated with bees which said 'honey', and some good books: *Are You There Bear?* by Ron Maris, *Can't You Sleep Little Bear?* by Martin Waddell and *Hairy Bear* by Joy Cowley. We stood back and admired our creation. This really was going to be a lot of fun. I went home excited, my imagination already 'working overtime'.

Enter the children

The next morning the children arrived, greeting old friends with enthusiasm and this new teacher with scepticism. I led them up to the classroom where they unpacked their school bags, chatted, had a nervous glance around the room and then gravitated towards the carpet where they, by force of habit, or training, sat down. No one mentioned, or investigated the black mass in the corner of the room. We started our Bear Hunt story straightaway and it was an immediate success. We read it through a number of times throughout the next few days, savouring the words and experiencing the illustrations which are so good that it almost seems possible to step inside the story. Soon everyone could join in reading the text. It gave the hesitant readers a tremendous morale boost with this new teacher, who might discover the 'truth' about their reading ability another day.

We set to work illustrating my displayed copy of the text and as they worked, gradually the children began to peep behind the black cloth. It was uncanny. Nobody shouted. The news went round like a Chinese whisper. First one went to look and then another, until at last one of the children came over to me and said, 'Did you know there's a bear in this classroom?' and I said, 'Yes.' They looked at me and grinned. The children seemed to glow with the pleasure of it all and that radiance stayed with them right through the year and beyond. A bright idea had gone right to the hearts of the children and the over-riding emotion engendered was love.

Joanna

For about a week, Joanna, the child who would not speak, watched. I had decided not to force speech on her, but to wait for her confidence to develop. I talked to her but never invited a response. She began to relax, to smile, to touch. Then one day she crawled into the cave and began to speak to the Bear. This was repeated three or four times a day. She would stay with him for about five minutes and Bear would smile at her and hug her. It might sound as though I have launched into a complete flight of fancy, but that is in fact what she did; snuggling up to the news-paper-stuffed suit, putting the floppy arms around her, and telling him the things she would not tell anyone else. I used to watch and listen, but from a distance. I am a good eavesdropper. It's a very valuable accomplishment in a classroom. One day I noticed a difference in Joanna's speech, a uniformity in her words, a rhythm . . . she was reading. There she was sitting on the Bear's lap reading *Hairy Bear* fluently, closely followed by *Can't You Sleep Little Bear?* I looked into the cave. 'Did he like the stories?' I asked. 'Yes, he loved them' she replied. I crossed my fingers, took a deep breath, and asked, 'Will you read me a story?' Joanna smiled, nodded, moved over and I crawled in with her and Bear. Fortunately peace was reigning in the rest of the room. From that day on her confidence grew, along with her ability to communicate verbally with me. She also began to talk a little with her classmates. They had become accustomed to ignoring her, not through any kind of malice, but with the matter-of-factness of six year olds. 'Well, Joanna doesn't speak' is what they used to say, but not any more.

It was, I think at this point that I realised that there was a powerful force at work in my classroom.

Out of the cave

One morning when the children came to school they were delighted to find that the Bear had come out of his cave and he was sitting in the large comfy reading chair. He had a book on his lap, but it was the wrong way up. They were amused and concerned, 'He doesn't even know which way up the book should be,' said one beginning reader. We talked about it, as we talked often about this business called reading, and they decided that 'it' just hadn't happened for him yet and perhaps we should help him. I watched with amusement as they took on my role as facilitator; selecting a big book, making sure that he was listening as well as looking. They would read him the story pointing to the words, and then go back to the beginning and play word games with the text. These sessions always attracted a group of helpers, usually the less able readers, who willingly joined in to help Bear read, thus helping themselves, by reinforcing their word knowledge and deepening their understanding and fluency. He made good progress, but never chose to read anything at night that was beyond the capability of the weakest reader. I talked with the children often about how this 'reading thing' happens, telling them that for some strange reason some children read before others, just as some crawl, walk, roller skate, ride a two-wheeler bike, skip, swim and grow tall before others.

Teaching the Bear to read was fun, learning to read themselves became fun too. For most of the slower starters the pressure had been relieved by the presence of our Bear, who was always behind the weakest of them.

There were, however, three children whose reading development worried me. One was Ann, the only girl in the class who had not begun to read. She felt that she was different to her friends and therefore needed careful handling and observation. David had a sister experiencing problems further up the school and his mother had decided to teach him to read her way, using a totally phonic approach, and a regime of instruction that involved half an hour a day of hard 'no nonsense' work. Then there was John, who had no phonemic awareness, a hesitancy in his speech, a poor memory and many reversals in his attempts to write.

... and into literacy

When I was busy, Bear would 'listen to the children read'. He never had to stop a story to deal with another child or to sort out a crisis. He was never in a hurry, he never suggested that a word was easy, or that the child should 'sound it out', he just kept right on smiling and enjoyed every book. Over the year he must have heard hundreds, some of them over and over again. I was able to stand back, to observe and to eavesdrop on these sessions. Sometimes two children would share a book with Bear. Often the partnership would be a strong reader and a weaker peer. They helped each other to become more fluent and more confident.

The level of phonemic awareness was an area that concerned me. We therefore collected and learned rhymes that we thought would amuse the Bear. One particular favourite was:

Teddy Bear, Teddy Bear,
　　Turn around,
Teddy Bear, Teddy Bear,
　　Touch the ground.
Teddy Bear, Teddy Bear,
　　Go upstairs,
Teddy Bear, Teddy Bear,
　　Say your prayers.

As they chanted the words someone would help Bear to do the actions. It was a rhyme not only spoken, but also written clearly for all to see. We looked closely at the rhyming words. We noted the letter pattern in 'ground' and saw that 'round' is the same, but in 'stairs', 'prayers' and, for that matter, 'bears' it is different. What a silly language English is, so we have to look closely and try to remember. Whilst all this phonemic reinforcement, for those who needed it, and visual awareness training, for those who were ready for it, was going on, we spent a considerable amount of time each day, as a class and in small groups, sitting around the easel watching and listening whilst I modelled writing. Children need to be talked through how to cope with difficult spelling and to see how competent writers think about their writing. They need to hear those inner conversations we have with ourselves, 'one c, two s's in necessary, or is it two c's and one s?' If all they ever see is adults effortlessly dashing off letters, as they struggle to cope with the 'thank you' variety, it is no wonder that they feel inadequate to the task.

Many of these children needed a lot of time to practise, and they needed meaningful topics to motivate them to write.

Bear provided the purpose

Exercise books, and sheets of lined paper can be very daunting to the early years writer, and often to writers of any age, so paper of various sizes, colours and shapes was on hand. We even had some Bear shapes. We started to quietly raid the art store for thin sheets of coloured painting paper, which we cut up and made into little books, again of different shapes and sizes. 'Bear bubbles', our version of speech bubbles, were particularly popular because they allowed the child who couldn't write very well to have a finished product that they were pleased with. I drew pictures of the Bear in different poses and venues and the children would select any one and write in the speech bubble. There was also another reason for their success, which I will return to in detail in the second part of the book. This is where I set you, the reader, a challenge to see if the 'penny drops' for you more quickly than it did for me.

A variety of speech bubble sheets were always available, some with just the Bear, others with the Bear and a friend. Soon the children were creating their own which they photocopied and added to the box. They also decided that they wanted some real books to write their stories in, so we made individual 'Bear Books' which were kept on the book stands next to the 'real books'. They all liked this arrangement and enjoyed reading each other's books, thus establishing an audience for their efforts. Having used the word 'efforts' I pause, because the lasting memory of that year was one of 'effortless' learning. I don't mean to belittle the children's work, but they wrote because they wanted to, with pleasure and enthusiasm. I don't remember having to cajole anyone.

Out of the classroom

In our school the class assembly was a feature that instilled fear in many teachers, probably because the parents were invited and it was seen by some as a testing ground where comparisons abounded and reputations were forged or crushed. In a school where consistency of approach was established, there seemed to be no rules, even time didn't seem to be of importance. Performances would frequently overrun into playtime, smart teachers opting for playground duty on Wednesdays.

With a sinking feeling I broached the subject of our impending trial to the children. Instantly one little voice piped up, 'It's no problem, we'll tell them the story of Edward Bear.' So that is what we did, we dramatised the original story and because we all knew that Edward Bear wouldn't be able to chase the children back through the forest and the river and the swirling grass, one of the children acted his part. Nobody ever said 'he's not real', we all just covered for his inadequacies. On the day of the performance one little boy announced that his Mum had said that Edward Bear could sit with her to watch the 'sembly. So there we were, doing our show, with the Bear sitting on the lap of a mother who had not been known for her involvement before.

The assembly was a success. Well, we all enjoyed it and the children spoke up beautifully because they wanted the Bear to hear every single word. At the end all the parents wanted to meet the Bear. It was all their children talked about when they got home from school. One mother said, 'They are having so much fun, and doing so well too.' The magic seemed to be stretching out from school and into the homes.

After that Edward started to get out and about more. He visited the playground, watched a PE lesson, he couldn't join in because he didn't have his kit . . . and thoroughly enjoyed being allowed to go to music lessons.

There was one memorable incident that I have to share. The phenomenon of separate toilets for boys and girls is something which young children entering school find strange. After all, at home everyone uses the same toilet, and the actual toilet itself is pretty much the same whichever house you go to. Little boys aren't allowed to pee against the tiles in the bathroom at home, so why should they be allowed to at school? As with all children there was a lot of giggling and sniggering outside the toilet doors. When the Bear started to go 'walk about' and before he adopted the name and gender of Edward, there was a discussion one day about which toilet Bear should use. The conversation progressed to a really quite sensible talk about the differences in the facilities. The girls, for example were intrigued with the concept of urinals, so, having first checked that there was no one relieving themselves, I suggested that maybe the girls would like to go and have a look at the boys' toilets and the boys could visit the girl's. This was all quite serious and orderly and would have gone off unnoticed had the Head not been showing round a party of important visitors at the time. My heart hit the floor. '. . . and what are you all doing?'

asked one of the bemused and I suspect rather amused visitors. One child immediately spoke up, bless him, 'We're doing research.' And then he went on to explain about the Bear and the need to research the facilities. At this point the visitor grinned broadly and said, 'Well, you'd better all get on with the good work.' The writing that came out of that incident was terrific!

'I luv U all'

I thought it would be a rather good idea to get Bear writing to the children, so one morning, after some kind soul had left him a small piece of chocolate cake for the night, there was a message on the blackboard;

Fnk U 4 the brn hny

The children thought this was great and stood around trying to make out what it said. 'Thank you for the' was easy 'brown honey', was a bit more difficult to figure out, but caused a lot of amusement when the children realised that it was chocolate. This simple idea was the beginning of a new era in the Bear's education because the children decided he needed to be taught to spell. They gave him lessons during the day and he practised at night. His misspelled efforts each morning gave us a language focus for our easel sessions. They all got very good at analysing his errors and showing him the correct form . . . with the desired outcome that they became focused on spelling too.

The same thing happened with letter formation. Bear was obviously forming most of his letters incorrectly so I asked a child with whom I had spent many unfruitful hours to sit down with Bear and show him how to write Edward correctly. Lo and behold, the stuffed Bear suit succeeded where my patient attempts had consistently failed.

I kept going into the staff room at the end of the day and saying that I was having the most amazing year and it had got nothing to do with my skills as a teacher but more to do with this inanimate stuffed bear suit.

Teaching Bear to write his letters correctly.

Everybody has a birthday

At the end of September, the two-year-old sister of Matthew died. Bear was invaluable as poor Matthew spent a lot of time cuddling him and gaining silent comfort. At about the same time Emma's parents split up and her father went to live far away. She read to Bear every day without fail, shared her lunch box with him and also her horrible emptiness.

Something had to be done, we needed a diversion from all this unhappiness. So when Bear's message one morning said,

'Wot's a birfdA?'

we decided that he should have one. It was agreed, I don't quite remember how, that Edward Bear would be six on October 6th. Plans had to be drawn up. In small groups of no more than four, the children discussed the finer points of a good birthday party. Date, time, venue, food, drinks, games, prizes, invitations, presents, cards, were all talked about with enthusiasm. The next day they worked in groups on the menu for the party lunch. Quantities had to be worked out, shopping lists drawn up, costings made. We were involved in mathematics activities for days on end. Children who showed little enthusiasm for 6 + 2 = were enthusiastically working out how many loaves of bread we would need if everyone had a round of sandwiches using two slices of bread. Children were going to the supermarkets after school and at the weekends with their parents in order to count the slices of bread through the plastic wrapping and then coming to school to share information. They researched the price of honey and peanut butter and asked their mothers to estimate how many jars we would need to buy. They filled empty Sprite bottles with water and sloshed it around as they filled paper cups to see how many cups there are to a bottle. At the end of each day we talked about the hard work we had been doing, the mathematics, the writing, the talking, so that they gave their effort the value it deserved. When we eventually had a list, everyone had to research the cost of one item so that we could then work out how much money everyone would have to contribute. The letter to the parents requesting the money and asking permission to go on an outing to the local supermarket was not only written, but also photocopied by the children. Their computational skills astounded me. They even sorted out the shopping lists so that we had groups of five with the same amount of money to spend. They managed all of this with ease, and on shopping day one group was ecstatic to discover that peanut butter was on special offer so they had cash in hand.

They made invitations, having first researched what to include, designed excellent birthday cards, and made small presents. The

great day arrived and I went to school with a slight feeling of trepidation at the thought of a birthday party from 9.00 a.m. to
3.00 p.m. BUT, it was a magical day. The children had planned it,
done all the work and now they all joined in to make it a success.
The first three hours of the day were spent shopping and preparing
the food and when all was ready, the party began. Surprising things
happened. Bear received cards and small gifts from all around the
school and a particularly lovely honey pot from the school secretary. People kept popping in to wish him a happy birthday. This all
added to the children's sense of well-being. It was as though the
adults who chose to step into the fantasy were rewarded with a
new sense of trust.

The parents became very involved. I had never had so many vol-
unteers offering to help before. One mother made a wonderful

Bear's birthday cake.

cake, with her daughter's help because Elizabeth had insisted that everything had to be done by the children. The helpers were amazed at how well the children behaved. What was the secret? Ownership. It was their day. And Bear? Well, he just sat there beaming as usual, loving all of them equally and never showing favouritism to one or two particular friends, which is often the death knell of birthday parties.

Bear facts

We started to collect books about bears as the children were interested to know more about his needs. We had big sheets of paper for them to write down details, along with the title and author of the source of the information. I have to admit that I was beginning to panic a bit and wondered how this could all be sustained. When somebody discovered that bears hibernate through the winter it seemed like a solution. Now we had a problem because we didn't know where he should sleep. Our classroom was rather small and there was a lot going on. Fortunately, someone came up with a bright idea and it was decided that he would sleep in a hammock suspended in the corner of the room. His cave had long since been dispensed with as he lost his shyness and spent more and more time with the children. So with the help of the leader of the school's Cub pack, a hammock was constructed. Bear's eyelids had been getting heavier and heavier, due to some quick stitching after school, and one morning when they came in he was in his hammock with his eyes shut tight. We found him a blanket and Matthew brought one of his sister's teddies for him to cuddle because she didn't need it any more. And there he slept for three months.

The area beneath the hammock evolved as a 'cosy area' where children could go and curl up with a book beneath the sleeping Bear. From time to time I would turn him over before the children came into the classroom in the morning, which amused them. They found 'sleepy' rhymes and lullabies, to write and they decorated the area with them. It soon became known as 'The Sleepy Corner'. This was a class who really loved playing with words.

One little girl pointed out that our Bear was in fact 'high-bear-nating'; quite incredible perception from one so young. So the Bear slept, through all the flurry of Christmas plays and parties, through the holidays and into January. On the 13th January the school photographer was due in school. The children really wanted Bear to be on their class photo, well, by this time his name was on the register after all. So I promised the children that I would ask, and if it was OK we would wake Bear up.

The gentleman in question had the ability to take the most beautiful photos of children but he was extremely gruff, short-tempered and impatient. Any out of the ordinary requests were usually met with scowls. Anyway, I decided to ask, tried to explain the significance and got a grunt of acceptance. I had sneakily stitched a pair of Bear's drowsy eyes on him that morning and turned him so that he was facing the wall. Luckily the children didn't notice. When we trooped down to the playground for the session, six of the children carrying the drowsy Bear, there was a total personality change in Mr Photographer. He was almost ingratiatingly pleasant. He kept referring to Bear as 'the furry gentleman' and took ages getting the arrangement just right. I have to give him due credit. He was magnificent. Bear had such a warming effect on people and he brought out the good that in this case was usually deeply hidden. After the photo we went back upstairs and Bear went back to bed, because he was all 'floppy and sleepy and couldn't even sit up'.

It's time to wake up Bear

Towards the end of February the children were getting more and more excited about Bear waking up. In fact many of them had been trying to aid the natural process as this lovely whimsical story, which mixes fact with fantasy, tells:

> We tried to wake him up.
> We put him on a tractor.
>> Cut down a tree.
>> Combed his fur.

Shone a torch in his eyes.
  Read a noisy story.
Made a volcano under his hammock.
  Tickled him.
But Bear went right on snoring.

We washed his fur on him.
  Sang a song.
  Shouted WAKE UP.
Tickled him with two feathers.
  Sprayed him with water.
But Bear went right on snoring.

We hit him with a bommy knocker.
Made a terrible sound with a racing car.
  Let go of balloons.
  Put earrings on him.
Let a squeaky mouse run on him.
  Then,
James' Mum just then brought in,
  A lovely big cake.
Bear sniffed, and WOKE UP.

This story, written amidst waves of giggles, by three little boys, very much follows the pattern of Lynley Dodd's delightful book, *Wake Up Bear*. In fact, the noisy story that they refer to is that book. We really did have a cake, which was a great treat. My birthday is the 29th February and has always been a party day wherever I have taught. The children thought it so funny that I have had so few birthdays. They would say, 'how many birthdays old are you?' I would tell them and then by multiplying by four they could work out my real age. It was all good incentive for mastering the 4 times table. I decided that we'd let Bear wake up when he smelled the cake, but as with the photo session, his eyes were going to be a problem. Before the children came to school that morning I took off the sleepy eyes and sewed back the 'wide awake' pair and then turned him so that he was facing the wall. I just had to hope that again nobody would notice. Fortunately they didn't.

Bear has to catch up

The children were so pleased to have him back with them, but they were worried that they had made so much progress and he would be behind. So they set to work making little books about all the things he had missed. As a form of summative assessment this went further than any written attainment test. They remembered details of all the things we had done whilst he was asleep. When the parents came in I was able to show them exactly what their children had learnt about magnets and electricity, light and sound, etc. The 'light' was particularly good because we had used prisms to make rainbows with the afternoon sunlight that came streaming through the classroom windows. One day we opened the class-room door and managed to made a rainbow on the corridor wall so that all the children passing by walked under it. That was a very good day.

So the year progressed with Bear continuing to support and stimulate the children's learning. They were nearly all reading really well now, and their writing was better than anything I'd achieved before.

From time to time I would worry that we were living in too much of a fantasy world, but these children knew that Bear was only a stuffed suit really, they were all happy and learning so much. Surely believing in him was infinitely preferable to believing in violent characters that bombarded them from the television screen.

Crisis

Towards the end of the summer term some of the children began to show genuine concern that they would be going to a new teacher soon and what would happen to Bear. We discussed the possibility of him staying with me and my new class, but that was not at all popular. They didn't like the idea of other children having their

Bear. Then a sensible soul said, 'Well, it's all right, he can come to primary 3 with us.' By this time we all knew who their new teacher was to be, so three of the class went to talk to Mrs Wiltshire to see if she would mind having another pupil. They told her that he worked hard but was not as good at reading and writing as them, but they assured her that they would help him. She willingly agreed and Bear's future was assured. In order to make his transition smooth it was suggested by one of the children that all our lists of letter patterns, and 'everyday spellings' should go to the new class teacher too. They also sent a number of Bear's favourite books, both stories and reference books. This, they said, was to help him feel at home quickly. Of course this gave the less able children a wonderful start with their new teacher. We had never passed on such material before, but really it was such an obvious thing to do. All my language-related charts went with them and the slower readers were assured that there would be books in the new class-room that they could read with confidence.

The children were delighted to see him on their return to school in September, but after a few weeks he received a fax from a relation in Yellowstone National Park, USA, inviting him for a long stay and a winter 'sleepover'. So he wrote them a note and left, just at the right time.

Chapter 2

'Where begot, how nourished?'

After the successful year with the Bear I was eager to try again, but obviously with a different character as the Bear was still very much in existence in his new class. I was deeply aware that the whole experience had been successful because it was so very different. Most new incentives that are tried with wholehearted commitment are successful. The true test comes in successive attempts when there is a danger that the project will lose the zesty tang of freshness and the experience will sink into a routine.

One of the successful features of the 'Bear Year' was the degree of ownership that the children had over the direction of their learning experiences. I followed, exploited the potential and capitalised on their lead. My planning dealt with the skills and knowledge base that I wanted the children to master within the school year. The choice of vehicle that would take us to that destination had to be influenced by the interests, needs and personalities of the group of individuals I was working with and my skill as a teacher to guide them competently on this stage in the journey of learning.

Bear had been great, quite literally, but his bulky size meant that he was very much a school phenomenon, he couldn't go home with the children. One of the unexpected benefits of the previous year was the bond that strengthened between home and school. The parents became more involved in what was happening in the classroom. The children actually went home and talked about the Bear and what he was doing. Inadvertently they were talking also about their own learning and the parents swiftly caught on to the fact that they could get a complete summary of their child's day by simply saying, 'How was Bear's day?' I vividly remember an incident when I was a very new, young teacher. I had to leave school early to attend a meeting and fell into step behind a group of children and their mothers. Spotting a boy from my class, I admit that I quickened my pace in order to eavesdrop. I just caught the mother saying, 'What did you do today?' as they walked along hand in hand. We'd had a good day. I'd spent all the previous evening planning and producing materials. I was poised waiting to hear him recount a stream of positive, enthusiastic details. All he said was, 'Not much, we just played about.' I felt like intervening and saying, 'Hang on a minute, what about . . .', but there was no point. The child didn't realise that the activities of the day were anything other than normal. School was behind him for the day, the best part, going home, holding his Mum's hand with the possibility of a detour into the sweetshop was important. From then onwards, I would draw the school day to a close by saying, 'Today you have all worked really hard at this, this and this,' in the hope that the children would not only be more aware of their own learning, but would also be able to repeat it ten minutes later! I recount this as an amusing anecdote, but summing up learning is important in any situation whether it be with five year olds or with postgraduate students.

What next?

The needs of this new set of children were different. I was going to take on a class whose reputation for 'liveliness', even at this tender age, went before them. There was also a high functioning autistic child whose behaviour could be bizarre. This time I wanted the character to help me with the development of the children's self-discipline because I believed that academic motivation would follow closely. I was stuck for an idea, the Bear had just happened as a result of lucky circumstances. I knew that I couldn't force it, that something would turn up.

I decided to wait and see what happened in the first days of the new school year. I was also very uncertain about how the autistic child would handle a classroom situation where imagination was at the heart of each school day. Autistic children are supposed to need routine and order, not surprises and high excitement.

So the school year began quite routinely, then one afternoon, before the children went home, I picked up Ingrid and Dieter Schubert's book, *Little Big Feet* to read to the class. They loved the story and roared with laughter at the antics of the tiny witch who flew around on a toothbrush rather than a broomstick. She was always getting into trouble, just like the majority of the children in my class!

The illustrations bore a strong resemblance to the 'troll' dolls that were so popular that year. It would be possible to transform a troll into an exact copy. So, straight after school I headed for a toy shop, bought a troll, some green wool for her hair and that evening Little Big Feet was created in as close a likeness to the book illustration as possible. I made clothes that exactly matched the illustrations and even managed some boots with the toes turned up. Even her toothbrush was the right colour and style.

The next morning when the children came into the classroom, there she was, hanging upside down, swinging on the easel. As Susannah put it: 'We have a little witch in our class. She popped out of a story book.' Once she 'was begot', her influence upon the children had an immediate effect. They started to write about her right away. At first the writing was descriptive:

We have a little witch in our classroom she has green hair stripy socks black dress and yellow pants with red spots.

As her quite awful personality developed, so the children began to write more imaginatively. To encourage such a response and to 'nourish' their enthusiasm, Little Big Feet began to hide whenever the children went out of the classroom. There was an eagerness to see where she was each time they returned. She was usually found somewhere quite inappropriate and had often caused a problem. For example, she might be found at the painting easel, having painted a messy picture. Once we found her sitting on a paintbrush presumably trying to make it fly. Another day she had built herself a house with the bricks and was hiding inside. The children just giggled and we wrote about what she had done.

Possibly the most memorable event occurred after a week of constant moaning on my part about the state of the toy boxes. The tidying up was not being done very well to say the least, and we had a general mix up of Duplo, Lego, building blocks, toy cars and sticklebricks in each of my carefully labelled boxes. Something drastic had to be done. Little Big Feet's particular skills were needed.

On a miserable, drizzly, Monday morning I arrived at school really early and set to work. All the toys were tipped out of the boxes in heaps all around the classroom. Paint was spilled, books pulled off shelves, chairs up-ended. The room looked like a tornado had whirled through. Little Big Feet was hanging by one of her pointed toes from a 'washing line' of paintings that crossed the room. As a final touch I left the room and locked the door, knowing that I could get back in through the connecting classroom when necessary.

I went to the playground to collect my damp children and, as I led them into the school building, someone rather whimsically said, 'I wonder what LBF has done?' They were certainly in for a surprise. We lined up outside the classroom to wait for the stragglers and then I said, 'OK, in we go.' The door wouldn't open. We tried again. No, it was well and truly locked. I asked one of my 'liveliest' little boys if he would ask the teacher next door to let him go through her room, so that he could get into our classroom and open the door. He shot off and a few minutes later threw open the door with a look of absolute delight on his face.

'You'll never guess what she's done now,' he yelled, 'Oh my God, it's awful.'

We all went into the classroom and there were 'wows' of horrified delight! What a mess! People passing by in the corridor were told to come in and see what she had done. Our Deputy Head, who could always be relied on to say exactly the right thing, came in and shook her head in disbelief.

'What are you going to do?' she said.

'Tidy up,' said Chloe, the autistic child, and with that they all

'You'll never guess what she's done now!'.

hung up their school bags and tidied up like I've never seen children tidy up before, or since. It was done quickly, sensibly and efficiently, accompanied by lots of giggling, tut-tutting and mutterings of 'naughty girl'. It really didn't take very long and when they had finished they all sat down on the carpet and we had a quite spontaneous discussion about what we were going to do about 'it'. The children were all totally unanimous in their agreement that she could not be left alone in the classroom overnight any more and certainly not for a weekend. She would just have to go home with someone every afternoon. This was a quite delicious idea. I could see the children savouring the possibilities.

'I don't think your parents would like having her to stay . . .' I suggested, keeping a very straight face. Dismayed silence followed.

'We'll write a letter to our Mums and explain.'

'We'll tell them that we'll be responsible.'

'We won't let her be too naughty . . .'

So we wrote a letter, telling the Mums most of the story. As with the letter that went home about the Bear's birthday party, the children wrote it and then arranged the photocopying.

Bearing in mind the importance ownership played in the previous experience, the arrangements for the little witch's trips home were organised by the children. They decided that she would be uncomfortable travelling in their school bags, so they searched around and found an old basket, which was just the right size. There was then the problem of who was to take her home first. We sorted this as a group work activity. The children worked in groups of four, with large sheets of paper and coloured pens. They talked and made notes and then came together to share their ideas. Children need to be the ones to sort such things, for the element of fantasy is stronger in them. They decided that the order for the following week should be decided on Friday afternoon before home time. This gave them and their family time to plan. It was also an exciting way to end the week. Planning just for the week ahead kept the element of anticipation which young children love. Knowing that your turn will be in twenty-nine days time makes the waiting too long and by the time the magic day arrives it can be a bit of an anti-climax. They so rightly thought of all these obvious points, that I might not have considered if I had meticulously planned everything.

Apart from the note, the children obviously prepared their parents well. For, from the first visit it became obvious that the parents were enjoying the fun too. On her first trip, she used Patricia's mother's lipstick to write a message on the bathroom mirror. This was the first thing the child saw when she stumbled into the bathroom in the morning and the simple message caused enormous pleasure. It was, of course, told to the rest of the class as soon as we were all in the classroom and then we recorded the mischief in words. This was either done by me, modelling with the children sitting around the easel, or by the host child who would write a personal account. Whichever method was used, we had a permanent record, which was made into a book. I will just share some of the entries.

When Little Big Feet came to my house she broke the Lego and then she got a jigsaw and took the pieces out of the box. Then she went into the kitchen and went into the cupboard and she opened the cereal packet. Then she poured all the cereals out.

When Little Big Feet came to my house she bit my dog's toe. My dog howled. She ran into my bedroom and hid under a big hanky. When I woke up I saw my dog with a red toe. We had to put a band aid on it.

When Little Big Feet was at my house she ate Grandad's cake. I found her in the fridge with green icing all over her face. She tried on my roller skates and crashed into the curtains. She didn't think they were very nice after that.

When LBF came to my house she was very naughty. When she went to bed she woke up and jumped on her toothbrush. She zoomed off into the bathroom. In the bathroom she filled the sink with water and she jumped in it.

This was a rather unfortunate happening because she came back to school soaking wet and the ink from the felt pens that I had used to colour her striped socks and polka dot underwear had all run. I suggested that I should get her some replacements, but the children looked at me in horror. We compromised on her having a school uniform. She was an evolving personality, clothes and all. So she stayed the way she was and during the year became more and more unkempt, much to everyone's delight.

Something interesting was emerging from the children's writing. The mischief which was taking place in the homes was, for the most part, initiated by the parents. They quite naturally, without being asked, entered into the fun and made strange things happen during the night. All, that is, with the exception of one home, which became obvious when the child reported back:

> When Little Big Feet came to my house she tipped out all the Lego. She didn't do anything else she just sat in her basket all the time.

Tipping out the Lego seemed to be her opening, warm-up activity wherever she went and I think that the child just wrote that to save face. There was not a lot I could do, other than to have a word with the mother before LBF's next visit to that particular home. On the other hand one of my boys took full advantage of the potential offered by LBF. He wrote:

> When LBF came to my house for the weekend she was so naughty that my Mum said she must never come to the Day's house ever again.

I spoke to his mother and it would appear that she wasn't really too cross. Her 'number three son' had been up to some pretty awful tricks in the name of LBF. She relented about the second visit but didn't feel she could cope with a whole weekend again!

Interesting developments were taking place relating to the behaviour of my group of loveable miscreants. At the beginning of the year I would be faced with a constant stream of complaints about their behaviour in the playground, in the library, in the toilets. Even in the classroom they were exhausting. After a few weeks of LBF's presence the complaints tailed off. Classroom incidents were few and far between. I think that what was happening was a reversal of all the advice I had ever heard about behaviour modification. Normally, troublesome children are given a better role model to help them improve their own behaviour. What I was giving them was a *worse* model. LBF did all the naughty things they would love to do, and more. They could share the fun vicariously and not get into trouble at all. In fact they could self-righteously point a finger and say 'Just look what she has done now,' whilst at the same time thoroughly enjoy the mischief. There was absolutely no need for them to dream up ways to liven up the days, LBF did it for them. Similarly, the Bear's appalling spelling and inability to read were a worse case situation, which had a beneficial consequence.

As the parents got more and more into the spirit of LBF's visits they began to plan special occasions to coincide with her visits. There was almost an element of competition to see who could come up with the best ideas. Of course, the children reaped the benefits as they were sharing the fun of learning with parents who might otherwise have been focused on the more academic aspects of their children's schooling. The Little Big Feet Book therefore included accounts of trips to the cinema, restaurants, theme parks, family visits, even grandparents were pulled into the fantasy. One parent was particularly imaginative. She was the instigator of the birthday cake in the fridge incident, which incidentally was accompanied by photographic evidence. On another occasion LBF was found sitting on top of the grandfather clock, which had mysteriously stopped at midnight, the witching hour. This mother was such an ally, not just through her creative imagination when LBF was at her home, but also because of her influence with the other parents. She very quickly saw what was happening with her son's learning acceleration and she encouraged others to throw themselves into the fantasy with their children. As the year progressed the parents became more involved in the written accounts of LBF's

'We found her in the fridge'.

visits, especially if they were weekend visits. One little boy, who had shown little interest in writing, was working really hard at home with his mother so that when it was his turn to write the chapter in the book, his writing would be really good. Great motivation and purposeful learning were taking place with a helpful, supportive mother.

As with the 'Bear' year, I was having fun too. Children are such intuitive creatures, they pick up feelings and emotions through senses that for many people seem to dull with age, or maybe those senses are just not stimulated enough to be sustained. I was happy and thoroughly enjoying my work, they picked up my feelings and were happy, relaxed and productive too. Thinking back to my first teaching post and my first Headmaster, I well remember an incident when my class had been rather unruly, he looked over his half glasses, as I do now with my students, and said, 'Each class reflects its teacher, Jennifer.' I suppose he was right, though at the time I felt aggrieved. The children and their teacher, in both these classes incorporating high levels of fantasy, were secure, happy and self-motivated through the sheer pleasure of learning. We were a team and I was a resource. The 'nourishment' was humour with a large sprinkling of mischief, resulting in learning that was such fun.

Chapter 3

'Reply, Reply'

It seems almost scandalous to me that experiences so integral to our growing up as make believe and fantasy can be so systematically ignored by my colleagues.

(Jerome Singer, 1973)

In this chapter I want to take time to look at what others have written about the importance of imaginative development in young children, in order to piece together the jigsaw of events that took place in those two classrooms.

Eight years before the 'Bear' made such an impact on my practice, I was researching the reading process as a preliminary investigation before introducing a more natural approach throughout the school. Someone recommended Sylvia Ashton Warner's book, *Teacher* which was first published, not in her native New Zealand, but in the USA. I found it inspirational, especially her view that reading should be motivated by the 'deepest springs of meaning in the human heart'. Working at the time from a traditional look and say approach, she provided her Maori children, at their request, with the words that most deeply moved them, words from the centre of their fantasies. At the time I didn't realise the significance of the fantasy element in her 'organic' approach to literacy learning, it was only as the Bear got under way that I returned to her work and read it with new insight. It also occurred to me that what I was harnessing was the power of love, unconditional love.

Searching for explanations in the literature proved to be rather hard. Hall *et al.* (1990) explain this dearth by suggesting that many academics and experimental psychologists would say the realms of fantasy and imagery are not areas that can be observed objectively and so, while they have been discussed, they have not been studied in depth. One of the few pieces of research on fantasy was in the treatment of disturbed patients. Jones (1969) points out that when looking at the power of the imagination, the therapist's first concern is the anxiety it can create. The teacher, on the other hand, sees the potential for human learning in the development of creative thought.

Imagination + Loneliness + Helplessness = Anxiety

The result for some people can be the need for psychotherapy. However, when viewed from the educational perspective:

Imagination + Community + Mastery = Creative Learning

This second equation matched exactly what was happening in my classrooms. Those three elements, *imagination*, provided by the characters, *community*, being the social structure and secure environment of the classroom and *mastery*, the very specific skills training that the children were getting through direct teaching, were definitely resulting in *creative learning*. If I had taken away one of those elements, the experiences and results would not have been so intense and would in fact have resembled the normal equation present in most classrooms. It's a bit like trying to cook a classic recipe without some of the ingredients. The outcome is a palatable meal but not a memorable gastronomic experience. I find that analogies with cooking come to mind so quickly when I'm talking about teaching. There are such direct similarities. We have to be careful that our schools don't become factories for bland mass-produced products. There must be room for multi-grain, wholemeal, wholesome, whole language bread! I seem to be getting a bit fanciful here, but I will pick up this theme later.

Psychologists such as Freud (1959), Lewin (1935), Piaget (1932) and Luria (1932) have all made reference to the fantasy play of children being the origin of adult daydreaming and other forms of thought. Werner (1948) spoke of the oscillation between fantasy and reality that typifies children's play, and saw this as being a necessary part of the child's development. The older the child becomes, then the more the child is aware of the fictitious character of his fantasy play. The Opies (1969) who took on enormous research projects centred on the playground, found that children are actively engaged in fantasy play up to the ages of eleven and twelve. I have only tried this sort of work with very young children but there are obviously possibilities for sustained fantasy experiences with older learners. It is what happens of course in role-play experiences; put learning into 'real' situations and it becomes more meaningful.

Chukovsky (1963) maintains that the imaginative powers of children are unstoppable. He examined what happened when a country rich in stories and myths tried to rear a new generation of children on total social realism. He tells of a Russian teacher, Stanchinskaia, who decided that her son was to be protected from fairy tales, the fewer harmful fantasies the better. She kept a diary of her son's upbringing and wrote that the boy began to spin the wildest fantasies from morning to night, as if to make up for the fables from which he had been deprived. He pretended that a red elephant came to live in his room. He became a reindeer with the first snows of winter and had an imaginary tiger which he carried lovingly wherever he went. Chukovsky concludes that:

> It makes no difference whether or not the child is offered fairy tales for, if he is not, he becomes his own Anderson, Grimm, Ershov. Moreover, all his playing is a dramatisation of a fairy tale which he creates on the spot, animating, according to his fancy, all objects – converting any stool into a train, into a house, into an airplane or a camel.
>
> (ibid., p. 120)

The child's notion of story and what is real and what is unreal was researched by Arthur Applebee (1978) who asked children of five and six years old, 'Where does Cinderella live?' They all believed in her existence, but few thought that she could actually be visited. They all believed with reservations, the believing was in their minds, in their own personal thoughts, they liked the idea of going to visit Cinderella but knew that she was in a special place that did not belong to the real world. When I interviewed the 'Bear' children two years later, one boy said: 'I loved believing in him then, when I was little, but not so much now at this age.' Another said, 'I knew he wasn't alive, but I wanted him to be, because he looked like he was and every day his eyes were moving.'

Mind you, these fantasy figures that have a physical form, albeit newspaper-stuffed suits, perhaps take a more believable role. I happened to bump into the mother of one of the Bear children some time after her child had moved on from my class. We exchanged the usual pleasantries and then she suddenly said, 'Where is the Bear?' I replied that actually he was in a cupboard, and she instantly retorted, 'I hope you've left the door open so that he can breathe . . .' I have to admit that I didn't quite know what to make of that and excused myself rather quickly!

I am aware that some of the work of Bruno Bettelheim is being questioned, but so much of what he wrote makes enormous sense to me. In his book *The Uses of Enchantment*, he argues that finding ourselves, finding meaning in our lives is probably our greatest achievement, and it comes, not at a given age, but with the acquisition of psychological maturity. The development of this wisdom, he argues, comes through the interaction of one's emotions, imagination and intellect, mutually supporting and enriching one another. He believes that our positive feelings give us the strength to develop our rationality and that is our hope for the future, that sustains us in the adversities we unavoidably encounter.

> If any one of these steps the child is taking in growing up could be viewed in isolation, it might be said that the ability to spin fantasies beyond the present is the new achievement which makes all others possible, because it makes bearable the

frustrations experienced in reality. If only we could recall how we felt when we were small, or could imagine how utterly defeated a young child feels when his play companions or older siblings temporarily reject him or can obviously do things better than he can, or when adults – worst of all his parents – seem to make fun of him or belittle him, then we would know why the child often feels like an outcast; a 'simpleton'. Only exaggerated hopes and fantasies of future achievements can balance the scales so that the child can go on living and striving.

(Bettelheim, 1976, p. 125)

I think that the Bear and the Little Witch gave my children the springboard to bring similar levels of imagination into the classroom situation. They certainly had a beneficial effect on a number of children with family problems. They also sustained the children who found school problematic.

It must also be noted that Einstein's powerful instinctive imaginings were the forerunner of his investigations. He insisted that imagination was more important than knowledge. How can one hypothesise without imagining, a hypothesis is little more than a scientific fantasy.

We sometimes assume that all children have an innate imaginative ability. Singer (1973) tells of two children swinging in a playground. One is imagining that he is an aeroplane. He makes aeroplane noises and then stops to refuel. His swinging has far transcended the actual physical situation. The other child swings for the purpose of improving his skill at swinging. He might be enjoying the sensation of rising and falling, but it is the first child who discovers the 'as-if' element, which seemed to be based on some experience carried in his memory and which involves some degree of imagery. Singer goes on to suggest that the tendency towards imaginative play can and should be encouraged in children, as it results in the interaction of constitutional brain capacities with a particular set of early environmental circumstances that provide stimulation and encouragement for practice. This is exactly what was happening with my children as they helped our Bear to read. The imaginative play situation provided the forum for sustained, repeated practice, which they desperately needed. I wonder whether this is what happens to older children who become hooked on books that appear in series. I remember as a child reading every Enid Blyton book I could lay my hands on from the Famous Five to The Secret Seven. Then The Bobsy Twins, The Chalet School and when I had exhausted those, I discovered some ancient copies of Angela Brazil and I was away again. What was happening in all of those reading experiences, was that I was immersed in a continuing fantasy experience. My own two children read their way avidly through Nancy Drew and The Hardy Boys. Again, they escaped into the familiar fantasy but the side-effect was that they were able to develop reading stamina through reading widely at the same level around about the age of seven or eight. It is at this stage that children are expected to make that huge leap from short stories to long narratives. When we deny children these texts and point them in the direction of books which adults think children should be reading, we are probably denying a large number of children the means to develop that precious reading stamina. Yes, we want children to read good books, but most of my generation moved on quite naturally. I have always believed that children have innate safety devices that shield them and protect them. We really should be looking at what children need, not what we think they need.

Singer also notes that children who are over-protected, who are constantly under adult supervision and are almost smothered with adult attention, may not develop fantasy skills for lack of practice. Such children may be as dependent on the adult to think for them, as they are dependent for physical care. A balance of parental contact and time alone seems to be essential to the development of a rich imaginative life. This is particularly relevant to our children today who no longer have the chance to play unsupervised because of parental fears for their safety. Who are seldom allowed to walk to school alone, jumping over the pavement cracks for fear that if as much as a toe touches the crack they will be swallowed up. Or that their bicycle has magical powers and if pedalled fast enough will take off . . . this was the way we went to school when I was a child.

Interestingly, children who are reported to be involved in considerable imaginative play also report greater closeness with their mothers. Could this include teachers as well? I think that was what was happening in my classrooms. That the relationship I had with these children was deeper than any I had had in my previous classes. I know that I kept telling my colleagues that I was having a wonderful year, and adding that, 'it's not because of me.' Margaret Meek's (1988) words, 'Any significant reading research I have done rests on my having treated anecdotes as evidence,' spurred me on. There were so many 'anecdotes' occurring that it had to be more than coincidence.

It is possible that the make-believe ability of children is decreasing in our factual, back-to-basics world. Television, video games and modern toys all provide the child with the ultimate in prefabricated, fantasy material, therefore can anything be left to the child's imagination? Singer cites Piaget who considered 'ludic symbolism', the make-believe fantasies of children, an indispensable step in their cognitive development. The imaginative symbol was the means by which 'the child moved beyond the concrete and immediately present, to the realm of operational thought.'

Singer (1973) describes a study of children in a New York kindergarten. Seventy first and second grade children (six and seven year olds) were closely observed in an individual play situation where they could choose from a variety of activities including toys, clay, paint and dressing up. An adult interactor was in the room with them as well as two observers who were unfamiliar with the hypothesis of the study. Throughout the play sessions the children were encouraged to tell the story of what they were doing. Singer felt that the results of the study showed that high functioning children are equipped with many of the cognitive skills which contribute to creative functioning. He cites Lieberman (1964) in her multiple correlation between playfulness and divergent thinking, who felt that the value of identifying such features as fluency, flexibility and joyful spontaneity in play, is that they provide, 'a clue to a similar ease of functioning when the child is faced with a more structured task that requires flow of ideas and shift of set'. This was exactly the case when my Bear children were faced with the need to research in books. They very quickly acquired the skills they needed.

One feature of Singer's study was that parents and teachers could assist children to develop fantasy by acting as models for them. Adults could say, 'Let's pretend,' and make up games and stories for their children. This is what I was instinctively doing with the Bear. By being a part of the fantasy I was modelling involvement for the children. We were all active participators. This observation links in with the work of Bandura (1977) who believed that children learn a great deal by observation. The child, then, in certain situations, is able to acquire patterns of behaviour without having to form them gradually by trial and error. Hall *et al.* (1990) also noted that the advantage that fantasy play as a technique has over more rational processes is that it is not dependent upon the normal stages of development for its effectiveness. In my work with the Bear this was particularly evident in the mathematics involved in the party preparations. The children were functioning far beyond their expected level of ability because of their inner motivation to solve difficult problems and also because the tasks were, to use Margaret Donaldson's term, 'embedded'. Valerie Walkerdine (1982) hypothesises that young children can reason when a task is thus embedded because they can examine what is permissible within the particular practice which is called up by the metaphoric significance of that task. She maintains that young children can reason in familiar contexts not because they possess reasoning 'skills' which are contextually bound but because the metaphoric context of the task allows them to examine the task within the boundaries of a particular practice. Thus by participating in the metaphor, the fantasy, the children were able to master the practices relevant to them. They wrote and they read because it was all within this realm.

While the writing of Hall *et al.* on 'Scripted fantasy in the classroom', deals with secondary students, their findings are relevant to my six year olds. They suggest that young children become deeply involved in fantasy because their imaginations have not been dulled by years of schooling which puts emphasis on logical, linear and rational thinking, whilst overlooking the creative possibilities of internal processes. They believe that teachers can boost self-esteem and promote respect between pupils by the use of scripted fantasy as a learning experience. Their researchers found that when pupils were engaged in such activities, a high level of motivation and energy was produced amongst the pupils. Children who had previously been reluctant to join discussions became contributors, as with Joanna who gained the confidence to speak because of the Bear. Their findings showed that the students also began to take more pleasure in their work, which produced a co-operative working atmosphere with an added improvement in the quality of written work. These findings had a direct parallel with the events in my classroom and children who had at first appeared reluctant to write displayed amazing progress in a very short time with the added dimension of the fantasy. Another finding that I found particularly interesting was that teachers who taught the classes following a scripted fantasy session found the children to be calmer and altogether more motivated to work. I mentioned in the introduction that I found the atmosphere in my classroom seemed noticeably different, that I had never been able to maintain the involvement on a permanent basis before. It is this quality to which they also refer. Atmospheres are not quantifiable, how can we prove the existence of this extra quality? Jones (1969) writes about teachers whose intuitions enable them to use emotion and fantasy in mastering subject matter, but who find it hard to explain to their colleagues how to improvise as they do. Jack Ousby (1992) whilst writing about reading and the imagination, pointed out that there is little research practice that will help us, we have to keep saying, 'does it make sense?' Well, it does to me.

Kieran Egan has written extensively on matters related to the quality of education and in particular has laid emphasis on the importance of the imagination. I want to close this chapter with a quotation from his introduction to *Primary Understanding* (1988a). If I have not succeeded in putting forward a convincing argument, then his words should push the reader to question what we do in the name of education.

The neglect of children's fantasy in writings and research in education during this century has meant the exclusion of an influence on curriculum and learning that has led to impoverishment and imbalance in schooling. Children's fantasy raises some considerable challenges to the principles on which typical early childhood curriculum is based. Those presently dominant principles seem to exclude much content that might well be included to enrich children's early years of schooling: they tend overall towards the prosaic and dull and exclude much intellectual excitement, and they fail to appreciate that fantasy is not an opposite of rationality but reflects the element that gives rationality life and energy.

(ibid., p. xi)

Chapter 4

Motivation to write

Musing

As I sit, poised to write this chapter about motivation in writing, I begin to think of the hundreds of times in my career that I have asked children to sit down and write. Did they view the blank, glaringly white sheet of paper with trepidation, or with eagerness and exhilaration? Were they excited by the prospect of their thoughts, their inner imaginings, their life experiences being caught and crystallised into words on a page, that others would share, with delight, with mild acceptance or with criticism?

I am suddenly aware of the feelings of all those children, and can understand the one who wandered the room searching for the right pencil. Who sharpened the point to the exact length. Who stopped for a chat with a friend. Who looked out of the window, apparently mesmerised by the world outside but who in fact saw none of it. Instead, using the normality of life around him, he drifted inwards to where the deeper thoughts dwell. Eventually, thoughts in place he returned to his place and started to write. For this is the stuff of daydreams, where some say creativity lies. So I've tidied my desk, made that extra cup of coffee, watched the clouds going by and now I am ready to begin.

Phonic knowledge and phonemic awareness

At the beginning of the 'Bear' year I had children who could write unaided and others for whom it was an arduous struggle. All the children had experienced 'instruction' in letter formation in their primary 1 year. This is when we introduced them to phonics, initially for writing rather than reading. I have used the word 'instructed' purposely because as a school we separated the skill of handwriting from the creative act of writing. So the children practised writing 'a' in the air with their fingers, with big fat paint brushes on newspaper, in the sand tray, with felt pens, with water on the tiled floor, etc. and all the time we were saying start at the top, curl round, up, down and a little flick makes 'aaaa'. The children began with the letters in their own name and worked out from there. The alphabet in both lower and upper case letters was available each time they wanted, or were asked to write. Venezky (1980) tells us that the ABC method, which dominated reading instruction for 2000 years, meant that children learned the letters and these were combined to make words. In effect, children learned to write and to spell before they could read. Bradley and Bryant (1980) extended this argument and suggested that for many children writing/spelling was the way into reading. They refer to beginning readers who could read 'light' but not spell it and write 'bun' but not read it. This seemed a logical way to approach reading with my large group of non-readers; building on their aural knowledge through their writing and their visual awareness through their reading. Clay, back in 1973 was saying that, 'for children who learn to write at the same time as they learn to read, writing plays a significant part in the early reading process'. Yet these skills somehow seem to have been pushed apart.

However, phonic knowledge is of little use if the child does not also have phonemic awareness. For we all know that a child can be trained like a performing parrot to say, 'a is for apple' but if he cannot hear, recognise, absorb and understand the 'a-ness' of A then he will not be able to apply the phonic training. Let me give an illustration of this. One day I was sharing a Big Book with the

children, it was called, *Rat-a-Tat-Tat* by Jill Eggleton. The text
goes like this: 'Rat-a-tat-tat. Who is that? Open the door and see.'
This repeated pattern is then followed by a series of monsters,
crocodiles and assorted nasties, who 'want to come in for tea'. We
read it through once and then on the second reading I decided to
play around a bit with the text. I said, 'rat-a-fat-cat' instead of rat-
a-tat-tat. This was met with peals of laughter from the children,
who said, 'do it again,' when the pattern next appeared. So I did
and then some of them had a go and we all laughed some more. I
suddenly became aware of a number of children who were 'laughing along' with the others but looking rather puzzled. They didn't
know what I was doing. They could all say 'r' for rabbit, or 't' for
teddy, but their lack of phonemic awareness made them oblivious
to what I was doing. These were also the children who had made
little progress with their reading.

This is a familiar problem that faces all teachers of young learners, the gap between being able to say 'a' and apply that knowledge
when writing or reading, for example, the word 'ant'. This is where
phonemic awareness comes into play and supports the child's
efforts.

Goswami and Bryant (1990) when writing about the importance of phonemic awareness found that children who had a
rich background of nursery rhymes, poems and jingles in their
pre-school experiences developed phonemic awareness more
quickly than those who hadn't. More than twenty years ago
Margaret Clark (1976) found that her 'young fluent readers' all
had a background of 'incidental' literacy learning in the pre-school
years. They came from homes where all the children were included
in literacy activities in a casual rather than formal setting. This was
the reason why we collected so many poems and songs about
teddy bears and spent time looking closely at the letter patterns
which formed the words. The 'Teddy Bear, Teddy Bear, turn
around', example in Chapter 1 gives emphasis to this urgent need.

Focused teaching/learning was done each day in short spurts
around the small easel. If I could only choose one piece of equipment with which to teach an infant class it would be my easel.
When I was at primary school, so many years ago, the blackboard

and easel were an everyday feature of classroom life. It was a seemingly enormous piece of equipment to a small child, and in my primary school was kept in a corner of the room. When direct teaching was called for, the easel was carried into a focal point in the classroom, the big wooden pegs put into the holes at the appropriate level, and then the teacher would lift the blackboard and stagger across the room, dropping the board onto the pegs and muttering about the chalk residue that had been transferred to her clothing. For reasons no doubt of safety and convenience, these rather cumbersome pieces of equipment gave way to wall mounted 'green boards', although they were still referred to as blackboards, and now to white boards which can be written on with pens, thus avoiding all that chalk dust. However, I think that inadvertently, something vital was lost. The old easel could be arranged at any place in the classroom for specific teaching with one group of pupils and it could be lowered so that children could write on it at an appropriate level. Even to this day I go into classrooms and see small children reaching up on tiptoes to write something on the very bottom of the blackboard. A blackboard which is no longer the sole recipient of the specific, direct teaching of the moment, as its very size means that segments are covered in messages and other information. In some classrooms there were even two, which stood like mesmerised giraffes amongst the throng of smaller beings. In New Zealand and Australia the concept and teaching value of the easel were not abandoned. Small versions were produced that teachers could use with children who would be sitting on the floor around the teacher. These then became the focus for Big Book reading and for the crucial modelling and direct teaching of writing.

Modelling

Children need these times of concentration when they observe a writer writing. The class teacher is the only expert they have, so we need to show the children how it is done on a regular, daily basis. It doesn't always have to be the teacher. Once the children are writing with confidence a child can sometimes model the writing. A child can offer appropriate advice because they are at the same developmental stage as those for whom they are modelling. It is also another way to motivate and encourage concentration. For many adults, unless we have struggled to acquire literacy skills ourselves, we have little real understanding of what it must be like to look at print and not be able to make head or tail of it. Our nearest experience would be to be a visitor in China, Japan, Russia or the Middle East and be surrounded by incomprehensible text.

I think there is a need to make explicit exactly what I understand by the term modelling. During the second year, when the Little Witch was going home with the children, some families really went to great lengths to create 'awful happenings'. The child would rush in the next morning eager to tell an audience who were receptive to listen and be amused. While the child told the story I would act as scribe, writing with a thick coloured pen on a large sheet of paper. Where a picture seemed appropriate, I would leave a gap. When the story was told we would then read together what had been written and then the fun began. Using different coloured pens the children would take turns to underline spelling patterns that we had already focused upon, e.g. the 'ing', 'ight', 'magic e', patterns. Or letter blends like 'st', 'th', 'ch', 'wh', etc. Another time I might focus the children's attention on punctuation and we would look at the use of capital letters, full stops and question marks. There was always a focus, we didn't attack everything at once. This was often whole class teaching where children engaged with what was relevant to their stage of learning. However, it became obvious that the very able children were absorbing much more than I had expected. This then was whole class teaching, which managed to reach out to the individual needs of a mixed ability group. Busy teachers often worry about how they can possibly meet the needs of all children. This seemed to be achieving that aim.

The big sheets of paper were then illustrated and stapled together so that we had weekly 'Big Books' being produced of the Little Witch's antics. These became the most often read texts in the classroom and were a valuable and inexpensive resource. The children's learning was progressing in a cyclical pattern of new challenges and reinforcement, carefully structured and supported

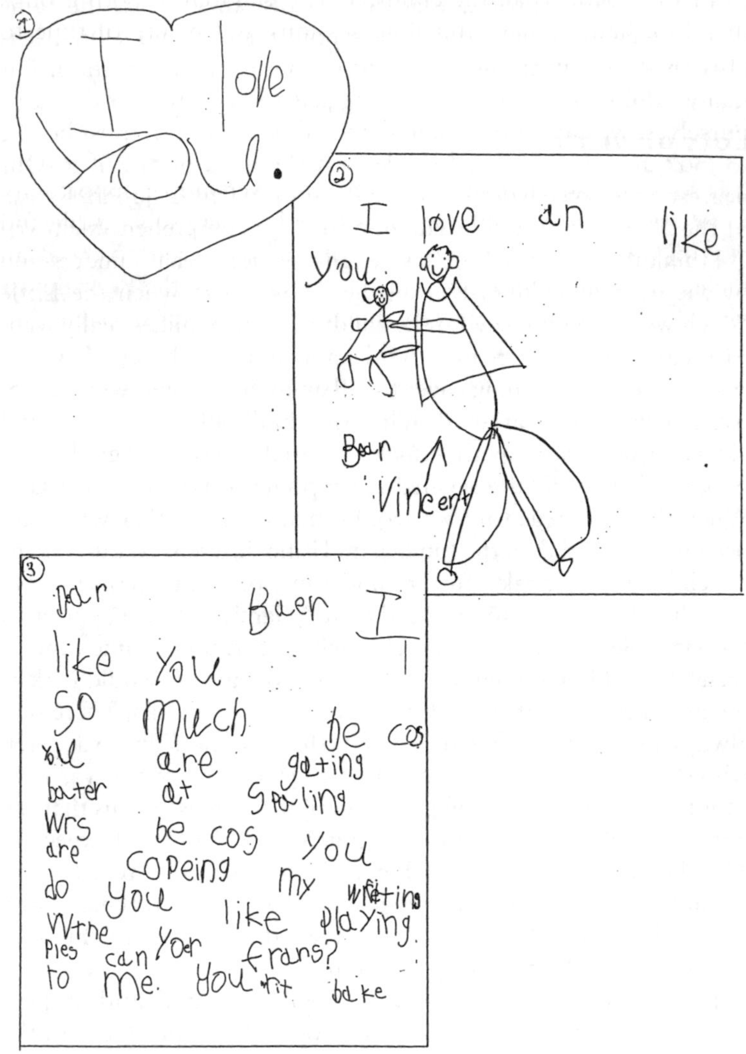

Figure 1 Vincent's early letters to the Bear which show his growing confidence as a writer.

to be of benefit to all the children. The children in both groups therefore had regular modelling sessions and plenty of time to practise for themselves.

Lots of writing

It is so important that young writers are given ample opportunity to practise. This is where the 'Bear Bubbles' were so valuable and also all the notes and letters that the children wrote to the Bear. Included is some writing by Vincent. He wrote to the Bear almost on a daily basis, unfortunately much was on scraps of paper, but here are three examples.

The first piece of writing is an unconditional statement of love. It was written in huge letters and filled an A4 sheet of paper. When Sylvia Ashton Warner (1980) was writing about her experiences teaching Maori children, she emphasised the importance of deeply felt emotions. She says:

> First words must have intense meaning.
> First words must be already part of the dynamic life.
> First books must be made of the stuff of the child
> himself, whatever and wherever the child.

'Love' is one of the most powerful forces that children feel, so they need the chance to write about love. All the children wrote this sort of message to Bear. Vincent then went on to say 'I love and like you.' Interesting, is it possible that this five-year-old child is aware that you can love but not necessarily like someone? He is making sure that Bear knows he is both loved and liked. Then the third piece is just wonderful. He writes:

> Dear Bear I like you so much because you are getting better at spelling words because you are copying my writing. Do you like playing with your friends? Please can you write back to me.

There is so much to look at in this letter. Always go for the content first. Vincent has recognised the power of modelling because he sees that Bear is learning from him, a more accomplished writer. It is a shame that affection seems to go hand in glove with achievement, that is something to store away. It is possible to infer that he associates praise with academic success now that he is at school. How many children feel like that? Maybe I'm reading too much into it. On to the proof reading stage and spelling analysis. He originally wrote 'dear' without the 'e' and put it in as an afterthought. He hasn't got the 'ea' pattern right in 'bear' this time, but he did last time. 'Becos' is a pretty standard spelling showing good use of phonic knowledge. 'You' was originally 'U' with the 'yo' added later. Evidence again of self-correction. 'Gating', 'Bater' and 'spaling' show that he is confused with the 'a' and 'e' vowel sounds. In 'wrs' he isn't aware of the 'o' or the 'd'. 'Copeing' is a fabulous try. We do say it like that 'cop-e-ing'. Well done, Vincent, for using the 'ing' pattern that we had been talking about. 'Yoer frens' again, 'yoer' is a really good attempt and 'frans' again shows this 'e' confusion. The final sentence is a plea, isn't it, and is completely readable, understandable and interesting in that he throws an 'e' on the end of 'bak' because he has noticed that 'e' is often used at the end of words. It is so useful to sit down and look closely at a child's writing, we can learn so much from it and it can inform our planning. I obviously needed to work in some activities to help with vowel sounds, particularly a, e and i.

Perhaps the real value of this kind of writing is that it gives young children the opportunity to express feelings. The 'I went to see my grandma on Sunday', followed by a picture, type of writing does not let the reader into the child's world and doesn't allow the child to say what he is thinking about. Is it possible that we need to look more closely at the genre we expect young writers to use?

Genre

When young children start formal schooling and begin to write, they are traditionally asked to write about themselves, their families, events of the weekend, retelling stories, etc., but are these the genres we should be starting with?

It was only some years later, when I was observing other teachers using fantasy figures in their classrooms that I fully realised what had been happening in my classrooms. In an earlier chapter I set the reader a challenge, now here we are at the 'penny dropping' point.

When these very young children wrote in the bubbles and scribbled notes, letters and cards, they were using the genre that they are most familiar with. They were writing conversations. They know about speech, they have been aware of speech since the day they were born, earlier possibly. Why don't we use this as our starting point? What usually happens when young children come to school is that we ask them to write accounts; 'what I did at the weekend' being an all-too-familiar death knell to creativity on a Monday morning. Or else we ask them to write stories, but how many young children nowadays understand story structure well enough to write it at such an early age? What they do know about is talking and the Bear gave them an opportunity to write speech down. Once they had gained confidence in this style they naturally progressed to experiment with other forms. They then went on to write simple stories for the Bear to read and wrote factual accounts of research about Bears. It might at this point be useful to look at some individual children.

Children writing

Nicola had a low self-esteem as a writer when she came into Primary 2. Left-handed, with poor fine motor skills, everything she attempted took a long time, exhausting effort and the results were messy. They infuriated her because they bore no resemblance to the stories that were in her head and that her elder sister could produce. The first example of her work caused a great deal of frustration, in the physical act of writing and her refusal to 'have a go' at the spelling. It had to be right. Around this time the Bear started writing messages to the children and Nicola particularly loved Bear's messy notes because they made her attempts look wonderful.

For Nicola, the Bear Bubbles provided the opportunity to write

Figure 2 Nicola's hesitant beginnings.

4

Edward Bear went
to the music i yesterday
and listened and watch
us playing games
and singing a song
and Mrs speed playing
the piano
and he was sitting on Mrs
tyrrell lap.
he saw outside Some people
going and Edward Bear
didn't know whether
or why they were
going out side so
he side sats here
Sohe gust sat there
ande watched
louder please.
Said Mrs speed
Edward Bear very
Cant hear well.

Figure 3 The day everything changed for Nicola and her writing.

an acceptably small amount and were casual enough for her to experiment with spelling by herself. Nicola became one of my first 'word detectives'. Due to her almost obsessive need for accuracy she would search out the words she needed. She found 'listen' and 'read' by looking around the room. I asked her to share this 'trick' with the rest of the class and this gave her self-esteem a real boost, just at the right time.

Example 3 was a breakthrough point. Now she was beginning to try for herself. She wrote this alone but asked for help with 'people' and 'sneaked'. It's interesting to see the errors with the vowels again as in Vincent's writing, a, e and i causing the greatest problems. It was such a pleasure to see Nicola's imagination coming through even in bite-sized pieces. And, then, one morning she came into the room with a look of fierce determination on her face. She took out her writing folder and with our support teacher, who was on hand for emergency assistance, she produced example number 4. It still makes me tingle after all this time. Where does a five-year-old child experience an expression like '. . . and Edward Bear didn't know whether or why they were going outside . . .' Presumably from the stories she has been told and read. What progress she had made in one month, and the stimulation was the Bear.

By January Nicola had become one of the most talented writers in the class. Her account of the incident with the photographer sums up the effect that the Bear had on everyone who came into contact with him and the depth of their caring.

> Mrs Tyrrell had to wake him up for our photograph because we didn't want him to miss our photograph because we love him. Mr —— was a jolly man. I think I like him the best today, probably because we had Edward Bear. But he couldn't go to the whole school [photograph] I felt sad because I would like him to go in it.'

She was such an observant little girl and so intuitive.

The little 'Bear Books' became a way for the children to notice

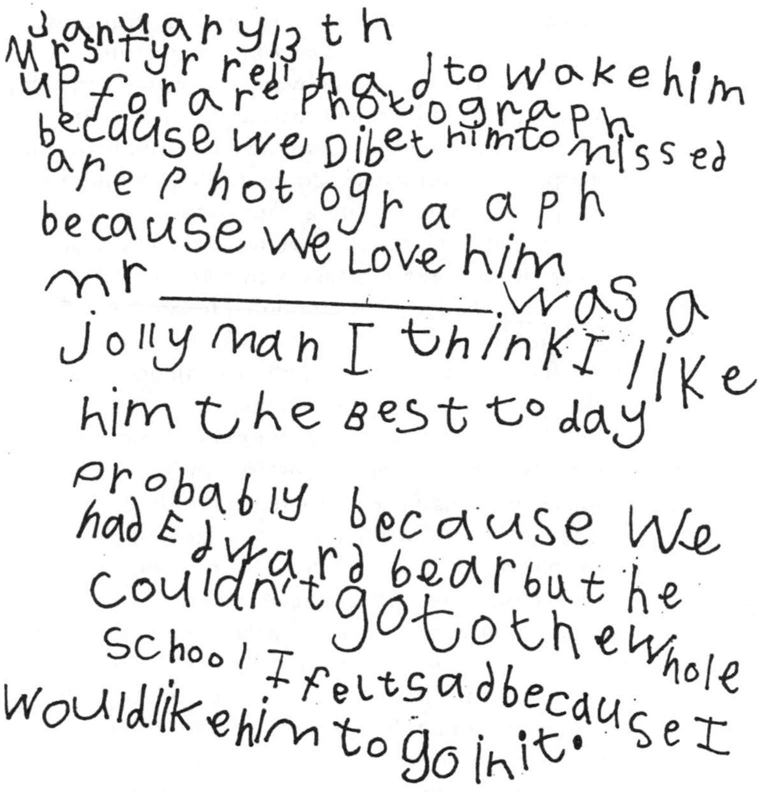

January 13 th
Mrs Tyrrell had to wake him
up for a re Photograph
because we Dibet him to missed
are Phot ograaph
because we Love him
mr _____.was a
Jolly man I think I like
him the Best to day
Probably because We
had Edward bear but he
couldn't got othe Whole
school I felt sad because I
Wouldlike him to go in it.

Figure 4 Nicola's deeply reflective writing.

their own progress. When you are six years old you are totally concerned with the 'now'. Some children fail to see their own progress, just that of their peers.

Vygotsky (1978) wrote about children entering zones of proximal development when they were able to achieve, in collaboration with a more experienced learner, what they cannot yet do on their own. He says that the teacher needs to be aware of these zones in order to lead the children into further learning. In a strange way I felt that I had not only recognised the zone but because of the shared excitement and involvement, I was in there with the children encouraging and extending their learning from within.

When I think back to that class, from the comfortable distance of time and in a peaceful, unstressed context, the enormity of the difference in ability was mind-boggling. Three years later the gaps had narrowed. Maturity was having an effect. The effect of a six months age difference was not so great with a group of nine year olds as it was when that difference amounted to one-twelfth of a life span of experiences at the age of six. All teachers of infants know this, many feel that they have to 'pull them all up to the same standard' by the end of two years, but should they?

The next child I have chosen to focus upon illustrates this. The youngest of three, with two older able sisters, Andrew was different. The precious son, he had been cosseted and indulged for four and a half years and then wham, school, grow up, perform, achieve. His fine motor control was a problem, holding a pencil for more than a few minutes was an excruciating effort even after a full year at school. Concentration levels were low, he was like an exuberant puppy who would roll around the room if permitted. We put our children into formal schooling so early, Andrew's life would have been so much happier if he had been born in Scandinavia where he could start school a couple of years later.

From time to time I would spread the 'Bear Books' out and have a look at them all. The cover alone told so much about the child and where he/she was. Look at these two. ' Bear Book' was written clearly around the room for the children to copy. Andrew doesn't even know where to begin, he has just copied the shapes of the letters, there is obviously no understanding of meaning as his reads, 'Book Bear The.' Look at his picture, isn't it wonderful? What an individual this little boy is. All his pictures of the Bear have huge tummies and big tummy buttons. Compare that with a girl of similar age. If we had a standardised attainment test for drawing a bear she would pass but I'm not so sure that Andrew would do too well. Perhaps if Picasso was the examiner Andrew would get accolades. By the end of September Andrew wrote the

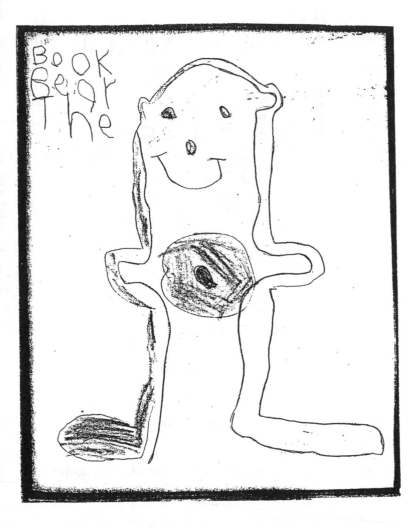

Figure 5 Andrew's 'Bear Book' cover.

Figure 6 Andrew's writing at the end of September.

following piece (Figure 6). A huge achievement, while the little girl quietly set too and produced this lovely addition to her book. Andrew could have been labelled as an under-achiever if we had to train the children to jump through hoops at the end of this academic year. Three years later he was directly on course. Time, support, focused teaching and confidence that he would get there in his own time, made it possible. Early bloomers sometimes shed their petals. Steady growers become strong plants.

Figure 7 One of the girls' 'Bear Book'.

Our Bear went to the hall and he Playd P.E with my Friend and me and it was Fun and it was a new beautifun and Pretty day and when Bear and my Friend and me we read a story book and he likes it.

Figure 8 Example of one of the girls' writing at the end of September.

The children wrote in their 'Bear Books' whenever they wanted to. It was lovely imaginative writing that exhibited their knowledge of spelling and syntax as well as possessing quality of content.

What about spelling?

Donald Graves (1983) stresses that children need to be able to write freely so that the pattern of their thoughts is not interrupted. Allowing them to attempt spelling gives them the opportunity to use words from their own oral language, which flow into their writing. Spelling is functional for it allows the writer to express meaning. Thanks to Nicola they had been encouraged to become word detectives, to try to hear the sounds in words, and to 'have a go'. This resulted in a few treasured incidents. As one girl was struggling to spell the word clock I knelt down beside her and spoke the word clearly several times. 'Clock, clock . . . what sounds can you hear?' She looked me straight in the face and said, 'Tick tock, tick tock.'

In my previous years teaching, as soon as the children were able to handle initial sounds they were given an alphabetically arranged 'word book'. If they needed help with a spelling they would find the page with the initial sound and then urgently pester the teacher for the spelling before they forgot the sense of what they were trying to write. I always found this problematic because of the urgency and immediacy of the need. The children would interrupt whatever was happening and often be told to wait a minute. The initial result was frustration for everyone. The long-term result of such practice was that the children acquired their own mini dictionary of words they had used, but there was no record of the child's development as a speller and more often than not the word they wanted was already in the book but they couldn't recognise it. As so much experimentation was occurring, I thought we would try a new method. Each child had a book with plain pages. A new page was started each week and the date was written at the top of the page. We called them 'Have a Go' books and they had to try for themselves first and then come for help, at least this way they didn't forget the word while they were waiting. If the word needed had a regular pattern like 'day', then I would subsequently ask, 'well, how do you think you spell "say"?' There was direct teaching going on, not just words on demand. Also, these little books gave everyone, teacher, child, parent an excellent record of spelling development. The children loved them because they could see their own progress.

When we gave the children a correct spelling we encouraged them to use Margaret Peters' (1985) visual method, 'Look, Cover, Write, Check,' but we added the instruction, 'Remember' after 'Look'. This way I felt we were combining the two views on spelling acquisition. Peters strongly believes that spelling is a visual skill, citing Bruner (1966) who suggested that children with high imagery were better than those with low imagery in associating words with pictures. This, Peters maintains, is very similar to spelling as it associates the look of a word with what the word depicts. Frith (1986) on the other hand, maintains that visual factors in spelling have nothing to do with visual appearance, but concern letter by letter structure, for the relationship of letters and sequences of letters within a word informs the speller. She believes that children begin to read by eye logographically but to spell by ear alphabetically. Read (1986) when studying children's first efforts in creative spelling, points out that they are strongly influenced by speech sounds. Young children can represent phonetic distinctions that most of us have ceased to notice. For example, the immature speller will use 'ch' instead of 'tr'. The 't' of 'trip' is not the same as the 't' of 'tip', it is more like the sound in 'chip', which is essentially 't' plus s/sh.

What I seemed to be noticing over the years was that most children do begin to write in this way. Then, around the age of seven, when their reading shows them the inconsistencies in the English spelling system, they develop and use their visual discrimination, thus supporting Frith and Read's hypotheses. Their phonic knowledge acquired for early writing then aids them with their reading, as they meet more challenging texts with unknown words. At this point the spelling of known words becomes automatic, the child can concentrate on what is to be written rather than how it is to be written.

How, then, to apply this knowledge in meaningful ways in the classroom? This is always the cry when working with teachers on in-service courses. They are happy to absorb the 'why' as long as there is a promise to incorporate the 'how'. The most successful sessions that I have been involved in both as a teacher and a facilitator, have been those where a practising teacher has come along to supplement the theoretical input with examples of recent, successful implementation.

Quite by chance the Bear's early attempts at writing gave me the opportunity for such practical implementation. I was able to focus the children's attention on very specific spelling skills in a way that held their attention through hilarious fun. As they laughed helplessly at the Bear's writing so they pooled their knowledge to aid understanding and then focused on the correct form. Again, as in the behaviour modification through a worse example with the Little Witch, I was instinctively using a bad example to help children to understand and improve. These children were becoming used to concentrating on words and word structure. They were seeing words in segments and as whole units and were very proud when they could spell a whole word 'without thinking'.

> Just as a reader comes to identify words as words, without reference to individual letters, so the practised writer commands a large repertoire of written word forms that he can put on paper, even by typewriter, without worrying about how they are spelled. The word is written as a unit, as an integrated series of movements. Such words are written much faster than if their letters were spelled out one at a time. Once again however, this is a skill that comes only through experience. You learn to write by writing.
>
> (Smith, 1978)

Cripps and Cox (1989) in their text, *Joining the ABC* emphasise the importance of joined writing actually aiding spelling. The children see and experience words as complete units and so the more they are written, the more automatic becomes the spelling. It makes sense. Children always used to be taught to write in a cursive style, it is only comparatively recently that 'infant print' was introduced in an attempt to simplify writing. This was possibly misguided. What it also meant was that children developed a style of printing, were getting to the automatic stage in their spelling and then, around the age of seven, they had to stop and relearn a 'joined up' style. This happened just at the time the children were accelerating rapidly and suddenly the brakes were slammed on. Hardly surprising that some children who had experienced a slow start then came to a complete halt and shunted into a siding.

Mr Pen

We started children writing in a cursive style as soon as they could form the lower case letters of the alphabet correctly, letters that is, that already had the joining 'flick'. They then moved on to practise joins in letters that are regular partners, for example, 'th', 'sh', 'ch', 'er', 'ing', and so on. This can be a rather tedious process and so I introduced another character that made the learning more fun. Mr Pen was one of those very big, fat felt pens. The cap very much resembled a hat and so I drew a face on a sticky label and stuck it onto the body of the pen. Thus Mr Pen came into existence. He was very much a Mr Punch type of character. He called the children by silly names so that Sophie, was Soapy and I was Mrs Squirrel. I made him speak in a harsh, Punch-like voice and the children used to sit and squirm with delight at the things he said. Maybe a module on ventriloquism should be a core feature of teacher education courses! Anyway, Mr Pen showed the children how to write the letters correctly and also how to join them together. He also had a 'packet of relations' named his 'skinny cousins' by the children. These were a set of thin coloured pens that we used to highlight patterns, etc. They, of course, spoke in very high squeaky voices and were always getting shouted at by Mr Pen for making a mess on his writing. The children loved them and listened attentively to everything they said. There was only one unfortunate incident when Mr Pen's ink dried up towards the end of the year, during a modelling session. Disaster. Somebody yelled,

'He's dead.' We even had some children in tears. I was frantically trying to remember where I had bought him, it, and wondered if I'd be able to get a replacement really quickly. Someone announced that you can't get refills for pens like that, which brought another wave of despair. It was strange how they swung from reality to fantasy, in and out, to suit the moment. What we did in the end was to promote the skinny cousins and Mr Pen was laid to rest.

Conventional writing

Children aren't silly, they know about conventional spelling. We need to make them see that we are helping them towards it. We need also to talk to children about times when conventional spelling is required. If we are writing a note home to all the parents, then it is important that the spelling is correct so that the parents can read and understand the message. This was agreed when the children wrote the note home telling their Mums about Bear's birthday party. If we are writing for the school magazine I firmly believe that this is a time when the conventions of correct spelling, grammar and punctuation need to be adhered to. The children can understand the reason and it makes understanding all the more possible. I have been involved in many heated discussions with colleagues over this issue in the past. It is one that each school needs to discuss and reach a consensus. You have to think about the feelings of the parents as well. To me, a five- or six-year-old child who writes 'becos' is displaying good phonic knowledge and applying it. To a mother or father, they just see an incorrect spelling and might not want the whole community to know that this is the spelling stage young Johnny is at. Sensitivity to the purpose and audience of the piece of writing is what is required.

This was the structure behind all the 'Bear' activities in relation to learning to write. The key to the children's success as writers was the emphasis on 'written conversations', linked to their obvious enthusiasm to write to the Bear. It was fun, it was purposeful and their furry audience was never critical, he always smiled and appreciated their efforts.

Chapter 5

Motivation to read

When will my child read?

For children and teachers in the early years classroom, the greatest source of pressure and anxiety is usually, 'when will the child start to read?' Parents get stressed, teachers try not to get stressed and of course the children sense the anxiety when people they love are concerned. Reading is such a difficult process to understand, how is it that some children pick it up effortlessly whilst others struggle painfully? I have only ever had one child articulate the experience amongst the hundreds of children I have worked with. When this little girl became a reader she told me that it was very, very scary. She had tried for so long to please her mother and me, had tried so hard to concentrate and then suddenly, as if by magic, she could read almost anything by just looking at the print. She didn't have to do anything. In fact, she couldn't stop herself from understanding print. She found it frightening. I'm not surprised. For a young child capable of that level of thought it would be alarming.

All children want to please. They soon realise when they start school, that reading is the one thing that their parents want them to be able to do as soon as possible. I don't believe for one minute that children make a conscious decision to avoid the acquisition of reading skills. Most children are happy to please those they love. So why can't they do it? Having worked with young children for many years and read everything I could lay my hands on to help me unravel the puzzle, I have reached a point where I feel I have enough understanding and confidence to at least cope with the mystery and support the children and their parents.

Margaret Clark's (1976) investigation *Young Fluent Readers* showed quite conclusively that early, effortless reading acquisition was linked to the children being brought up in homes where print mattered, long before they went to school. They all had a background of 'incidental' literacy learning in the pre-school years. They were all children who were included in literacy activities in a casual way. Fine, when they started school this made the teacher's job easy, they fed them little books to read one after the other and 'bingo' the children were reading. When I first went back to teaching after seven years at home with my own two infants, I was a support teacher for six months. I worked for two hours a week with each of the four primary 1 teachers and in each room I was asked to 'do the reading'. This meant that I sat in a corner, with a shoebox full of little books. I called a child's name, they stopped what they were doing, they came and read me the last two pages of the book, I gave them the next one, recorded the new book and that was it. That was the way I was told to do it, so I kept quiet and did as I was told . . . for a while! There was no time to talk, no choice for the child. Ask them what they were reading and they would say 'orange' or 'yellow' or 'blue'. These were not books about the colours of the rainbow, but colour bands on the spines of the book that labelled the child's ability to read. There was status and security for the parents in the 'colour band' their child was reading and this transferred to the children who saw it as a race through the colours. Sadly for some it turned into an obstacle race. I well remember my own son telling me proudly that he was reading 'brown'. He didn't know what he was reading, he couldn't remember the story, but he was reading 'brown' and that mattered. I could just as easily have been a monitor in a Dame school a hundred years ago. This 'Little Jack Horner' approach to reading seemed to work for 80 per cent of the children, but there were always four or five 'plums' who remained hidden in the pie and hadn't got a clue. They would often have mislaid their book, needed to go to the toilet and eventually sat down with sweat breaking out on their foreheads. We would then endure five minutes of excruciating misery as they guessed their way through a page. These were the children who perhaps didn't have a literacy rich background, or perhaps they just weren't ready yet, or perhaps they had some serious learning problem that this exercise would only exacerbate. I was lucky, in many schools the percentage would have been reversed and there would have been 80 per cent struggling and 20 per cent achieving. These are the children that we worry about. These are the ones who desperately need natural, 'incidental' ways to be formalised in the school setting, to help them to catch up. This was where the fantasy figures provided that missing element. The Bear and the Little Witch took the focus off learning and put it onto fun. The learning then became incidental.

I mentioned, in Chapter 1, that there were concerns with the 'Bear' class because of the large number of boys who had made little visible progress with their reading during their first year in school. I would have been more concerned if it had been a mixed group, but many boys do seem to take longer to settle to the formality of school learning and there often seem to be delays. It could have been that they had missed out on the casual literacy awareness that develops in the pre-school years. These boys were mostly the children of very busy parents for whom quality time with their children possibly did not include the incidental literacy experiences that occur when you do have plenty of time. Another possibility is that early reading material in school often concentrates on narrative texts. Stories are wonderful, but a more varied text exposure will offer children the chance to concentrate on areas of interest. Let's put more non-fiction books into our infant classes, providing of course that they are of an appropriate level. A few years ago this might not have been possible but there has been a distinct move in the right direction in recent years and publishers are now beginning to meet the need. I well remember one child who learnt to read with a football match programme. It was his most precious possession because he had managed to get the autograph of one of the players. He pored over it and eventually 'made sense of the print'. Alan Bennett, in *Writing Home* (1994), refers to his similar early experiences as a very young child.

I had read a few books by this time, as I had learned to read quite early by dint, it seemed to me, of staring over my brother's shoulder at the comic he was reading until suddenly it made sense.

I think that my own son became a reader in a similar way. We had a book called *Katzimir the Greatest* on semi-permanent loan from the travelling library. Once a fortnight we got four books each, but Ben renewed *Katzimir* and changed three. He could recite the text and whilst looking at it one day, things began to connect and he saw that the print on the page had a relationship to the words I was reading. He began to recognise some of them. He had begun to engage with reading.

It could also be the case that these children were just not ready to make those literacy connections just yet. Perhaps they just didn't have literacy maturity or perhaps it was a family pattern that had not been exposed.

Literacy secrets and cover-ups

These children with a delayed commencement in reading acquisition interest me so much. They are often highly intelligent. They are often following a family pattern of so-called reading delay, based of course on an institutionally perceived requirement that children should achieve literacy competence in direct relationship to chronological age. This occurs even in educational systems that stress the need for parents and teachers to be aware of individual differences and developmental variations. However, this 'family pattern' of which I speak is often hidden from the child (and often the other parent too) who therefore gets no comfort from the knowledge that Dad became a reader when he was seven and look what he can do now. Dad might not want to remember his early struggle, perhaps he expects the system to do better for his son and so he puts pressure on the child and the teacher, for the very best of reasons. Learning to read for many children can be an emotionally charged nightmare, which leaves scars.

A very good friend of mine has a son for whom early school

days were an unhappy experience. He didn't become a reader until he was nearly seven. At the end of primary 2 the family moved to an area where the boy's November birthday would have him repeating year 2. They visited the new school with the child saying nothing. They visited the classroom where he would be and the boy eventually let go of his mother's hand and slowly made his way over to the bookcase. He picked up a number of books and flicked through them and then returned to his mother. With a very solemn face he looked up and said, 'It's OK Mum, I'll be all right here.' He was all right because circumstance had given him space and a bit more time. He was also all right because when the mother recounted this story to her mother-in-law she was told, 'He's just like his father, he was seven before he read and then there was no stopping him.' Apparently the Christmas after the boy's father had started reading, he was given thirteen books as presents and he read them all before he returned to school. Grandparents are a vital link in this family reading pattern. They remember the details that will give enormous support to all concerned. They remember events that parents often suppress or choose to forget. Wouldn't it be a good idea if we could have grandparent interviews as well as parent sessions!

My own family are the reason for my obsession with early literacy. I have thought hard about the inclusion of this next section, it would be so easy to ignore my background, but it plays such a pivotal role in everything I have done professionally and was probably at the root of my understanding of what was happening during these two school years that were so different from all the others. So, with my family's agreement, I open up this closet of skeletons.

I learned to read with no problems. For me it began when I was four. I used to sit on my mother's knee after lunch and we would read the Rupert Bear section in the *Daily Express* newspaper. Mum read the prose part and then helped me to sort out the rhyming couplets. She also taught me to recite the 'Lord's Prayer' and to sing 'God Save the Queen' whilst she did the ironing. I suppose this helped to train my memory and there were certainly a lot of hard words for me to come to terms with. I think that was just about it. There were no playgroups or nursery schools in my day. When I went to school I remember vaguely some books with a shepherd and a sheepdog, but have no recollection at all of being taught to read. I just started reading.

That was back in the early 1950s when there weren't many books in my home, just the daily paper and my mother's library books. My sister, who was four years younger than me, couldn't do it. We had the same parents, the same background, the same experiences, the same school, the same teachers, I did it and she didn't. It caused terrible anguish and at that time all she got was, 'You must try harder, your sister can do it.' We all did everything we could to help, but she really didn't read with any confidence until around the age of twelve. By that time I was at the local grammar school and she at the secondary modern. A family ripped apart by resentment on her side, guilt on mine. I felt guilty because I was the one who could do it, but I didn't know why. We grew up, had children of our own, my sister's son started school and the nightmare began again because he started to experience the same problems.

Around that time I was talking to my father who was now well into his seventies and he suddenly said, 'Did I ever tell you about when we moved to Scotland and I went to secondary school there?' No, he hadn't, so he went on to tell me that at the age of twelve, in his first week at the new school, he had been made to go out to the front of the class and was told to read an extract from Robert Burns. He said that everyone laughed because of his stumbling attempt to articulate the Scots words with his English accent, but little did they know that he couldn't have read the words even in English. I remember feeling sick. I asked if he had ever told my sister. He said that he was so ashamed that he never told anyone. The pattern had gone through three generations. Now this was an extreme case, of probably a specific learning dysfunction, which caused a very specific self-esteem dysfunction.

From that point onwards I always asked the parents of children who struggled, very gently, if there was a similar pattern in their own childhood. There usually was. I asked them if they had spoken to their child about it. They seldom had. I suggested they should, for the good of the child. The response was always an implication that they must have been doing something wrong, or didn't try hard enough and they were determined to make sure that their child did it right so that they wouldn't suffer too. This of course just added to the pressure. When I suggested that perhaps they just weren't ready and neither was their child, they honestly hadn't thought of that. It was often the father who had experienced the 'problem'. Had they said anything about their background to their wife? More often than not, the answer was no.

What can be done about it? Well, we need to be open. We need to talk to parents about the reading process as often as possible and we need to encourage fathers as well as mothers to come to these sessions. We need well-trained teachers who are knowledgeable and confident. We need to create a classroom environment where children cannot help but make sense of print. We need to do this in as natural a way as possible so that no one senses failure because they can't seem to make connections as quickly as we would like.

Sharing and interacting

With this group of children I shared books with them at every opportunity and rather than have them all sitting silently, they were encouraged to interact with the text. They were, after all, very young children and I think that it is necessary for them to verbalise their feelings. This goes against the grain with many teachers who prefer children to sit quietly and listen to the story. We are here getting into the realms of discipline and control rather than optimising learning. This is a very real conflict in school, where we have so many dual roles and aims.

We read a wide variety of books and made a point of revisiting old favourites and we talked about what we were reading just as one does with the shared reading of a book with a child on your lap at home. As a teacher of young children we need to find ways to bring the natural ways of learning into the classroom. Julia Spreadbury (1993) initiated a research project in Australia, which focused on the nature of the adult–child interactions with a given text in the home situation. Her study highlighted the social nature

Sharing a book with a friend.

of the reading process. In all her recordings the child and the text sharer talked their way through the book and she concluded that this was a vital social construct for the child's later independent readings.

We therefore talked our way through many books. We also read over and over again the *Bear Hunt* book. Due to the fact that we dramatised the text for a school assembly, every child knew the text by heart. For my non-readers, connections could be made between the memorised text and the marks on the page and around the room. I think that this was a key factor in the development of their understanding in the same way that it helped my son with his *Katzimir* text.

Particular favourites

The children loved the shared story times and liked Bear to listen with them. We became addicted to the 'Teddy Robinson' stories in which I used a particularly growly voice for the Teddy Bear. From time to time I would use a similarly growly voice to encourage a child back on task. On one occasion a girl said, with complete innocence, 'Mrs Tyrrell, you sounded just like Teddy Robinson then.' When I was reading she was completely absorbed in the story, seeing it, living it, so my voice didn't belong to me, but to the character in the book. Children who have a rich background of story learn to use imagination in powerful ways. Stories are about inner feelings, emotions. Later in the year I introduced Maurice Sendak's *Where the Wild Things Are*, and they became completely involved in the story. They dipped in and out of the imaginary world that Max created to cope with his conflicting emotions, as easily as they switched out of classroom thought and into playtime activity when the bell rang.

As Holdaway (1979) said of children with developed imaginations:

> Because this behaviour is so difficult to study, its significance has almost been overlooked in the traditional teaching of literacy. Sentimental things are said about the magical world of literature and the imagination, but few think of applying this driving force to the basic learning of literacy tasks. Nor do they think of remedying the situation for those children who have not learned to operate imaginatively. For such children, half their motivation for becoming literate is paralysed, and so learning to read must be like learning to walk with one leg.

I had never thought of reading like that before, that it could be such a crippling experience without the ability to get inside the situation being described. I suppose I am like that when I go to see a play or film. I instantly associate with one of the characters and am a source of great embarrassment if the plot takes a tragic turn. For I weep uncontrollably. My husband says, 'But it's just a story.' I know that, but I am in it and can't understand how he can remain on the outside and unmoved.

Let's teach Bear to read

When I heard children reading to the Bear in his cave, I knew that I had to get Bear more involved. That is why he moved out of his cave and sat himself in the 'reading chair' one morning.

I mentioned earlier that the children started helping him. Through helping Bear, the weaker children got lots of positive reinforcement, which was exactly what they needed. In some schools older, less able readers, are encouraged to help younger children because this provides them with the extra practice at the right level. It is an 'everyone wins' situation. The same thing was happening with my boys but I was able to catch them at a younger age.

Talking to the children about the reading process

I often talked to the children about how this 'reading thing' happens. I told them that for some strange reason some children read before others, just as some crawled, walked, roller skated, rode a two-wheeler bike, skipped, swam and grew tall before others. I really don't think that we talk to children enough about the reading process, or the whole business of learning for that matter. They need to be included in their own learning far more and I don't just mean being allowed to read the 'year end' assessment reports. I was really not too concerned about these children, as the majority of them were still under six years old and dare I say it, I knew what I was doing. My confidence that they would make it was probably a key factor too. None of the children were picking up negative feelings from me. For be assured, children have highly developed sensory skills. They pick up and react to atmospheres, I don't know how they do it, but they do.

Being aware of children in need

Four children did worry me, as I mentioned in the earlier chapter. One was Ann, the only girl with any reading delay and who therefore needed close observation for a number of reasons, self-esteem being at the top of the list. David, who had a sister experiencing problems further up the school and whose mother had decided to teach him to read her way, using a totally phonic approach, and a regime of instruction that involved half an hour a day of hard, 'no nonsense' work. Matthew, whose sister had died and who therefore needed watching for many reasons. Then there was John who seemed to have no phonemic awareness, a hesitancy in his speech, a poor memory and many reversals in his attempts to write. He reminded me of my sister. Through the year Ann made steady progress and didn't outwardly seem to lose self-esteem. Of course there is no way of knowing for sure. Matthew coped and gained momentum towards the end of the year, which led him into a primary 3 year of leaps and bounds in progress. David seemed too weighed down with the stress at home to cope with the situation in the classroom. He was a very immature little boy and I think he was frightened by all the fuss. Unfortunately the family moved at the end of the year so I don't know what happened to his progress. John had definite problems and was referred for assessment and extra help.

The children who were already reading were romping along. My task was to keep those who had not yet got off the ground buoyant and positive so that they did not give up before they began. Stanovich (1986) in his article 'Matthew effects in reading' takes a quotation from Matthew's Gospel: 'For unto everyone that hath shall be given, and he shall have abundance: but from him that hath not shall be taken away even that which he hath' (XXV: 29). The implication here being that those who get off to an early start amidst praise and the glory of success, make speedy progress, whereas those who struggle sink deeper into despondency until a sense of failure takes over and hampers progress. One particular worry to me at the time was the provision, in the form of remedial help, for such slow starters. It would seem to be of the wrong kind. Often in schools, when children are selected for help, they are taken out of the secure classroom environment and are usually presented with texts that are linguistically poor, where the story line is less than gripping, and the illustrations are functional rather than additions aimed at firing the imagination. They work with a teacher who sees them for a limited time, miss what is going on in the classroom and know that they are labelled. I would rather have had someone working in the classroom with me, or teaching the class while I worked with the children in need.

Making the whole day a literacy experience

I don't want this book to make specific reference to any major national incentives, or fashionable practice, or contentious issues. They come and go, the good parts stick and are adapted and absorbed into good practice and the not so good ideas usually whither away. I did this work just before the Literacy Hour came into being in England and Wales. Much that was recommended was already a feature of the regular work that all teachers incorporated into their daily teaching in the school where I worked. Everything I have described could slot into that hour but I would take it further and recommend literacy days! I used every minute of the time I had with the children to promote literacy, because as I see it, literacy is the keystone for all further learning. Even in mathematics sessions we had to read and often write. Many people won't perhaps have noticed that when we form letters our hand movement generally goes in an anti-clockwise direction, but for most of the numbers they go in a clockwise direction. These things need to be talked about and laughed at because to a young child it seems a bit silly. There was a language of mathematics to be absorbed, a thesaurus of mathematical terms to become familiar with. For example, 'add on' can be expressed as plus, more, in addition, total. We needed to be able to read and understand these words in order to do the calculations. Then there was science, history, geography, all falling within the realms of language learning. I used every subject as a means to a literacy end. Our focused learning sessions around the easel were as likely to be modelling writing about magnets or oceans, events of yesterday or a lifetime ago. What better way to teach children about using the past tense than in a history lesson, or the precise language of detailed observation in a science lesson? It is the natural way to teach about genre.

Influences on my thinking and practice

The work of Liz Waterland (1985) and her apprenticeship approach to reading had a lasting effect on my practice. It came at a time when I had raised two readers of my own, as a parent and then sent them to school. In a home full of books I found myself sitting down after dinner to 'do the reading' and being faced with less than interesting texts. So, I am not afraid to say that it was '1, 2, 3 and Away' and we read something else. I then unashamedly lied on the reading card. When I suggested to the teacher of my younger child that I didn't think she needed to read through the sequence of the scheme, her reaction was intense. She was convinced that my daughter would fall behind the rest of the class without the structure of the scheme. If she was falling behind it was because she was so bored with the books she was ploughing through that reading had ceased to hold any pleasure.

Margaret Meek's *How Texts Teach What Readers Learn* (1988) also had a profound effect, especially her description of how Sartre taught himself to read from a text he already knew by heart. This rang all sorts of bells in my brain when I selected *The Bear Hunt* as a text to read and reread. I read all her work avidly and wallowed in the practical good sense of her words.

Selecting books

Our classroom was therefore full of tempting books by author illustrators, where text and pictures worked together to reveal the meaning to the child. Bruner said that the writer recruits the imagination of the child by presenting the familiar in a different way. Anthony Browne's books are particularly good at twisting the real with the unreal to produce stories and pictures that keep the children poring over the texts until every detail has been discovered, and still they find more the next day. I am quite sure that I have not found all the pigs in *The Piggybook* (1986) yet. We also had as many appropriate non-fiction texts as possible and lots of poetry. It sounds like a recipe, doesn't it? Well it was, with ingredients selected from a food cupboard equipped for a siege! The heart of our school was the library. We had huge numbers of books with multiple copies of texts that we found worked with readers of all ages. We had a teacher responsible for this library who gave hours of extra time, on top of her job as a class teacher, to selecting books based on reviews in the educational press as well as recommendations. Teachers could select armfuls of books, take them to their classrooms and renew and replenish them on a regular basis. Actually the children got involved in the renewal process. Every week we had a basket of books that, 'we could just about do without', but that didn't mean that we wouldn't choose them again another week. Old favourites were valued and welcomed back into the classroom. In this way the weaker readers could develop reading stamina with known texts, which gave them a foundation of confidence to go on and try an unknown book. Each classroom had book display units attached to the walls so that books could be displayed with the cover facing the browser. Covers to tempt readers just like in a bookshop.

Reading with children

When we read with children it should be a sharing time, not a time for the child to perform. We had large comfortable chairs in all the classrooms, large enough for an adult and one or two children. By sitting close to a young reader one can feel physical tension if it is present. More usual would be the action of a child wriggling as close as possible to share the physical and intellectual contact.

As I have mentioned earlier, Bear would often listen to the children read. He was a wonderful listener. He was totally unthreatening and very attentive. He never said, 'Hey you could read that word yesterday, why can't you read it today?' He just kept right on smiling and enjoyed every book and over the year he must have heard hundreds. I was able to stand back, observe and eavesdrop. Sometimes two children would read to him. Often a weak reader would team up with a more able companion. They helped each other to become more fluent.

Information texts

Books about bears were in abundance. As the children asked questions about his needs, diet, habitat, etc. we would always turn to a book to find the answers. They soon figured out that you go to texts with particular questions that need answering and by using the index, find relevant paragraphs without having to plough through the whole book. Lots of children haven't developed good research skills at a more advanced age than my little beginners did that year. Margaret Meek voices concerns about study skills and suggests that children are often given lessons in how to use dictionaries or library skills before they have a real need of either. Study skills, she says, can only be effectively learned in, 'a context of genuine enquiry, a necessary knowing.' We certainly had 'necessary knowing.' These six year olds found out all about the difference between a contents page and an index. They discovered the use of a glossary which all went towards making their quest for knowledge easier. Disturbingly, they also discovered that a lot of books for young investigators do not include such pages, there is probably an assumption that they are too young for such things. My children became very selective and dismissive!

I would often leave large sheets of paper and pens near the books so that they could make collections of Bear Facts. If someone found something interesting they would jot it down, with the title of the book and the author. Research with a purpose, reading with a purpose, writing with a purpose became a part of our everyday life. The beauty of this early 'research' was that they automatically wrote the data in their own words, often very briefly. When children are introduced to study skills later there is a temptation to copy large chunks of information. This needs to be discouraged or else they need to be shown how to quote someone else's work. This was one of the main criticisms of 'project work', children were kept busy producing presentable copies of information with often very little understanding of what they had read or written.

The reason that Bear hibernated for three months came about through their reading research. Underneath the hammock we made a sleepy corner, where we collected lullabies, favourite bedtime stories and words about sleep. They were constantly finding new words and adding to their collection. They were taking such great pleasure in words.

Slipping into reading

And so the children slipped into reading. Through concentration on skills teaching for writing, daily reading and performance of rhymes and jingles to aid phonemic awareness, concentration on phonic knowledge for writing in particular and reading when it helped the situation, modelling with Big Books, daily writing, lots of shared reading of a wide variety of good texts and the fun of the ever present need to make our very eager Bear literate.

Chapter 6

The whole child

In this chapter I will look at the effect the Bear and the Little Witch had on the learning and emotional development of a number of individual children. Often, when we analyse the effectiveness of our teaching, individual children come to mind who seem to have slipped through the net with regard to levels of motivation and interest in the work being done. However, with these two groups of children there was only one child who did not respond wholeheartedly. This child joined the class half-way through the Bear year and found it very hard to pick up the intensity of the feelings of the other children. Such children joining a class in mid-session often take time to settle in, for I have to admit that it was hard for a newcomer to step into the situations created. The rest of the children were drawn effortlessly into the fantasies and blossomed despite the fact that both classes had the usual mixture of abilities and needs. Amongst the two groups there were a number of children for whom the fantasy experience had particularly beneficial effects.

I am going to begin with Chloe, an autistic girl who was six years old. She was further hindered by the fact that English was her second language. It was Chloe's position and integration into the social structure of the class that were the main reason for the existence of the Little Witch.

Chloe

I have to admit that I was quite alarmed at the thought of absorbing an autistic child into my class. From the little I knew, autistic children need order and regular routines, not the high levels of imagination and the fantasies that I was developing with the children I taught. I had been told that she was classified as being a 'high functioning' autistic, but that did not really mean a lot to me. The first thing I did was to write to the National Autistic Society who were enormously helpful in sending me a range of booklets about the condition. I knew that her behaviour was, to say the least, bizarre so if I was going to continue my work with another fantasy figure I was going to have to select that character with great care. Having already decided to wait a while, I was able, during the first week of term, to observe her position in the class. It was very strange. It was almost like having a little robot in the classroom, who had been programmed to perform certain functions. Chloe could therefore line up silently, unpack her school bag sensibly, sit down on the carpet quickly and wait for the register quietly. Initially I wondered whether there was a problem with the rest of the children, not her! However, once the programmed routine was over her 'difference' became very apparent. She displayed classic behaviour patterns of repeated, obsessive behaviour. Every morning, after the register had been taken and the morning's work discussed, the first thing she would do would be to get all the little 'play people' and lay them head to toe along the edge of a bookcase. She also touched everything and everyone with her mouth. It was as though her senses were impaired and her mouth provided her only sense of feeling. In a way it was just a continuation of the way a baby 'tests' everything new, immediately putting it to the mouth. Perhaps she just hadn't moved on in her learning experience. In those early weeks I found myself watching and imagining the way she must be thinking. I tried to get inside her and to see and feel the world through her eyes. I began to touch objects with my mouth. The experience was definitely more intense. I could feel, smell, hear and also taste all at the same time. In a way I was becoming slightly obsessive about this special little girl and her particular needs. My family, however, thought that I was becoming rather strange. There was one memorable evening when I opened the door to some dinner guests and our friend had a new, very short haircut. As I greeted him I could feel myself wanting to touch his hair with my lips. This had got to stop or I would be getting myself into trouble!

I found that if I watched Chloe really carefully I could see a reason for most of the things she did. One incident, however threw me right off guard. I had moved the rubbish bin for some reason, I don't recall why, it was just one of those things you do without thinking. I watched in amazement as Chloe got up from her chair when she had finished her snack, walked to where the bin had been and dropped her crisp packet on the floor. Some of the children noticed and commented. I suppose what I should have done was to put the bin back where it had been and leave it there, but my instinct was to keep moving it and train her to look. Obviously I was not going to start moving everything around, just one thing at a time. It was at this point I started to think that I needed a character that would take the spotlight off Chloe's behaviour.

The story of Little Big Feet was the answer I had been looking for. Here was a character that got up to all sorts of mischief and could be manipulated to take the pressure off Chloe. Tidiness was definitely one of her fixations and I did try to make an effort in this respect. It was important that she knew where to find what she needed, so when the toys were constantly in a muddle, the Little Witch stepped in with her manic mess-up. Chloe's reaction was surprising, for she just stood in the middle of the room, turning her head slowly to take it all in and then she said very clearly, 'Mrs Tyrrell, better clean up.' The other children took her cue and as I described earlier, did an amazing job. Chloe was the leader, she alone knew exactly where everything should go. Her full integration into the class had begun.

As the children revelled in the antics of the Little Witch, they also began to appreciate and show compassion for the 'differentness' of Chloe. If the witch wasn't doing something to make them smile, then Chloe probably was. She became a very special member of the class as the children began to accept her just as she was. They were incredibly patient and protective and when she was not at school there was an emptiness that no one liked. One child summed it up by saying, 'Chloe just makes everyone smile.'

Autistic children often have advanced abilities in particular areas and Chloe had an incredibly retentive memory for spelling. We could be walking around the school when suddenly she would say, 'Mrs Tyrrell, how to spell music room?' I would spell out the letters, which she repeated and that was it, fixed in her memory. Of course, this made her an incredibly valued resource to my class of word detectives. It also provided her with the interaction she so desperately needed to prevent her from retreating into her private world.

Chloe's whole learning pattern had to be carefully programmed. Children's learning is usually cyclical. They learn and re-learn, building on and refining previous learning. Chloe, at the age of six did not seem able to do this. Once she learned something, then that was it, no need to refine or relearn. We first noticed this when looking at the drawings she had made of herself. There was no change at all over many weeks. Her drawing was at a very basic level. So one day my classroom helper sat down with Chloe and a mirror and drawing materials. They both looked into the mirror and talked about what they could see, then, a drawing was made based on those observations. Gradually she developed an awareness of the link between observation and the need to modify and extend her knowledge. The Little Witch helped because her appearance deteriorated over the year and the clothes she wore changed, due to the excesses of home visits. Chloe's drawings of the Little Witch therefore had to change too. She could see the physical changes in the Witch but not so easily in herself.

The Little Witch, whose behaviour was very like her own, seemed to give Chloe the chance to relax and feel secure within the classroom situation. On good days I was able to push her quite hard, making her respond, forcing her to stay in our world. However, one day she just had as much as she could take and a strange conversation evolved that went something like this:

Figure 9 Chloe's picture.

CHLOE: Mrs Tyrrell feels sick.
ME: No I don't Chloe.
CHLOE: Mrs Tyrrell feels sick. Go to medical room.
ME: No, Chloe, I'm fine.
CHLOE: Mrs Tyrrell feels sick. Go to medical room. Mrs Tyrrell go
    home.

She wanted to get rid of me and knew that children who were sick
would sometimes be sent home if they went to the medical room.
When I remained in the classroom she got very cross and drew this
picture.

Chloe's language was not making progress, again she seemed to
have acquired functional language in two languages and saw no
need to learn more. She had particular problems with pronouns as
you might have noticed from the snatches of dialogue already
included. In particular she would never say 'I', instead she always
referred to herself as Chloe in the same way that a two or three
year old does. I was able to make the Little Witch do the same
thing when she scribbled notes to the children. In our modelling
writing sessions we would write and frequently highlight or underline all the pronouns. The sheets of writing would be left on the
easel for the children to return to. Chloe seemed to learn best by
reading independently and she would often return to the easel and
read aloud, taking in the new knowledge. This approach seemed to
be successful as there was a definite improvement and extension in
her spoken language. Progress was slow but sure and steady.

When I asked this group of children to reminisce about their
primary 2 year, one of the things they always remembered was
when the easel fell over because Chloe was sitting underneath it
while I was reading a story. There were particular places in the
classroom where she would retreat to and under the easel was one
such place. Story times were always hard for Chloe, she could not
relate to stories that were being read aloud. I don't know how she
managed to knock the whole easel over, but I was very lucky that
there was no injury. Interestingly when I asked for specific memories of the Little Witch many children told me about things that
Chloe had done, thus proving that to a certain extent, I had

achieved my aim to integrate this very special little girl. As a result of her integration we were able to concentrate on furthering her learning.

Close, personal friendships were not really possible for Chloe, not that she sought such a relationship. All the children showed patience and understanding but there was one little girl who was drawn to her. Katy was also different in her own way. She was new to the school having had a less than successful start somewhere else. A fluent reader at this early age, she walked into the classroom, saw all the books and began to devour them. For a couple of days she did very little else but sit on the cushions and read, and while she read, she watched. The games and antics of the rest of the girls did not interest her at all. She seemed to have an aloofness and indifference to any overtures of involvement that were offered to her. She was, however, drawn to Chloe who she seemed to sense was a kindred spirit. They developed a kind of friendship that appeared to sustain itself through telepathy rather than words. They were able to look at each other and respond. This was particularly evident in the playground when they would frequently spend twenty minutes playing catch, running and laughing without any words being spoken. Katy was undoubtedly very bright, an exceptionally gifted child who was a misfit in the classroom. I have only come across a handful of children like this and they can very quickly be labelled disruptive, lazy, inattentive or insolent if their particular needs are not recognised early. They are also very difficult to integrate, as they need a different time frame in order to become deeply involved in what they are doing. Higher up the school this is possible, but in the normal hustle and bustle of an infant classroom, more geared to short attention spans, such a child can flounder. Katy found a soulmate in Chloe and the two children even began to make out-of-school visits to each other's home, something that Chloe had not done before. Thus a chain of events, triggered by the fantasy figure was having a ripple effect on the well-being of children who are often on the edge of classroom social structure.

Due to Chloe's presence in the class it was decided that the group would progress throughout the school without being split up and re-grouped. This was done with the full support of all the parents, which was particularly pleasing because they too had gelled into a supportive group, working in partnership with the school. This helped her enormously as with the exception of one or two changes she only had to readjust to a new teacher and class-room each year. Quite enough change for a child with such particular social problems.

Mark

Mark was also a member of the Little Witch class. He was a quiet, sensitive, serious and very shy child who hadn't shown any sign of starting to read by the end of his first school year. The second of three children, he had a mother who was very relaxed about her children's schooling and had the confidence to know that he would achieve in his own good time. The elder brother had a similar slow start and their mother felt this was going to be a family pattern. The home was full of books and story times were a regular evening event. I was not unduly alarmed because everything seemed to be in place. However, Mark was a child on my special care list who needed lots of literacy experiences and time to absorb the input. The top priority was to be careful to maintain his self-esteem, because Mark was fully aware that others were making faster progress than he was.

Mark adored the Little Witch from the very first moment. They just clicked. Here was a creature who did all the things that he secretly would like to do himself. There was no sense of embarrassment or fear of doing wrong which made him nervous if a friend transgressed, for Mark had a very clear understanding of the boundaries regarding behaviour and expected others to have the same standards. Young children have so many readjustments to make when they start school that I am amazed that so many of them cope as well as they do. I remember my own children making quite significant changes in the way they behaved at home in the first year of schooling. My son went through a phase of putting his hand up when he wanted to speak at meal times and he used to get so cross with us when we laughed at him. My daughter called me Mrs Mummy at school because teachers were 'Mrs' and I was a teacher in the same school. It is all a process of readjustment and for most children the desire to conform is very strong.

Mark just loved taking the Little Witch home and in fact he was the one who decided that she needed a basket to travel in to prevent her from flying around and causing mischief on the way home. He had an incredibly receptive imagination and this was exactly what he needed as a source of stimulation for writing. Children like Mark soon tire of writing for the sake of it, but he did need to write as often as possible in order to progress. He also had determination and good concentration and would sit frowning with the effort as he struggled to write the thoughts that were filling his head. As he articulated the sounds of the word he was writing, his pencil dug into the paper with the force of his determination. Mark was a child who definitely came to reading through writing, but in the early days he was not even able to read back what he had written. It used to make him so cross and he needed lots of reassurance to make him believe that it was going to get easier. Meanwhile the books kept going home every day in his book bag and his mother would share them with him at home. The interest was maintained and Mark came through the learning process seemingly unscathed, due to a strong partnership between home, school and Mark.

At the end of the year with the Little Witch I had a year's sabbatical leave in order to study for a higher degree at the University of Nottingham in the UK. While I was there I took the Little Witch with me because the children said that I would need some company. To compensate I bought them a small teddy bear dressed as Robin Hood and sent it to them. I had a whole bundle of letters thanking me for Teddy Hood, the most precious of which was Mark's:

Dear Mrs Squirrel,
How is University? We like Teddy Hood. I wonder how LBF is? We are sorry because the letters are late. Our assembly was yesterday it was about pirates. It was fun.
Love from Mark
I still like writing. OOO

Figure 10 Mark's 'OOO' letter.

I should perhaps explain the 'Dear Mrs Squirrel'. That's the name that Mr Pen used to call me. The children loved it, all good alliteration reinforcement. I was pleased that in February of the next school year he was still interested to know how LBF was getting on. The line that gave me the greatest joy, however, was 'I still like writing'. He still liked writing despite all the struggle and frustration. This child had such strength and would I felt sure go far in life. I'm not too sure whether the 'OOO' are noughts instead of crosses, or a sign of affection that didn't involve kisses!

There is one other incident which should be included for it gave me such a jolt and made me reflect about the quite awesome power we have over these young impressionable children, to encourage or condemn through the utterance of the odd word. With all the children I took every opportunity to praise outstanding effort and to

Figure 11 Mark's 'raindrops' letter.

talk with them about their writing. Not every piece of work would receive praise because too much ecstatic praise loses value and the children know that it is not deserved. When there was mutual delight at a piece of writing I would send the child to the office to ask the secretary to photocopy the work, so that parents and grandparents could share the pleasure. I must have done this with a piece of writing Mark did about a rainy day. Two years and two teachers later he wrote me this note as shown in Figure 11.

I wish I could find the words to describe the warm feeling that a huge grin inspires as it spreads right through the body. Just look at the confident handwriting, the spelling and punctuation, the presentation with the writing in a cloud and the raindrops falling around. Then let the content sink in. The piece of writing in question had been 'honoured' on the fridge door for more than two years. Dispel cynical thoughts about untidy kitchens because that would not be the reason why it had been there for so long. Mark's raindrop work was obviously a milestone. After initial euphoria I then passed through a phase of total panic. I had absolutely no recollection of the incident. Something as important as that in the child's development as a writer was a commonplace event which left no memory. What if I had been busy and hadn't sent him? What if I hadn't seized the moment? What if I'd been frazzled dealing with some classroom incident and had just passed it off? What if? What if? This is where quality time to reflect on the day is so important to the teacher. Time in which individual milestone achievements can be noted . . . but how often do we get that sort of 'serenity time' in which to ponder the events of the day or week?

Mark was a success story. He was a little boy who was very fortunate to be in a school with consistent patterns of teaching and an ethos of caring understanding. One last anecdote in this saga emphasises the everyday caring ethos I mentioned. It would not be uncommon for older children to wander back to my primary 2 classroom, to share with me the pleasure of a really good piece of work. When this happened I would always try to stop what I was doing and give quality time to the child. Whenever possible I would get the children to stop what they were doing for a few moments and join in the celebration. These visits benefited everyone. The older child would often talk to the younger learners about their learning journey. They gave encouragement to slower beginners who often wondered when it was going to happen for them. I'll never forget one day when a nine-year-old boy burst through my door and yelled, 'Mrs Tyrrell, it's happened, I can read!' Time to stop work and jump up and down with glee indeed. That had been a long hard wait, filled with hours of hard work by teachers helping him to get to this magical moment. Often children who struggle have lost so much self-confidence by the time they become readers that they almost fail to realise that they can do it. The activity is tainted from then onwards with the sour taste of prolonged failure. The whole issue needs to come out of dark secluded cupboards and be regularly aired. Success needs to be celebrated at whatever age the child achieves the objective and for the children who have struggled the cheers need to resound. This sort of sharing of success is good for everyone's morale, teachers included. As an early years teacher I have often worked really hard with children, building the foundations, for the next teacher to 'reap the harvest'. Parents who perhaps don't fully understand the process sometimes comment that their child got nowhere in Mrs So-and-So's class but now he's doing really well. Learning is an ongoing process with each experience building on the last. I have to admit though that there have been many times when I have wished that I could keep the children longer and be an active part of the success!

So to the last study. Here I look at two children who had horrendous personal problems to deal with during the year with the Bear. For children with problems at home, school can be a place where they lead a life that is as near normal as possible. It often provides a chance to be themselves and forget. But the problem is always there and usually manifests itself in some way or another. I was fortunate in these occasions to be fully informed by the parents. I well remember an incident in the early days of my career when I was summoned to the Headmaster's office after school one day. I was told that the father of a boy in my class had been into school to say that his son was very unhappy in my class and that he cried a lot at home about it. This was all news to me, we did not seem to have a problem and I was not aware of any conflict with other children. We agreed that the Head would come into my classroom to see for himself. Everything was fine, but still the father kept coming to school and with each visit he became more irate. This was very worrying and went on for quite a while, until one day we found out that the parents had just split up. The mother came to school and said that they had kept their problems from the children, but of course they hadn't been able to do that. Children are so perceptive of atmosphere, absorbing the problems and reacting in their own way.

Fortunately I was fully informed of the problems involving these two children in my 'Bear' group.

Matthew

Matthew's sister had been ill for some time before she died. She was only three years old. He knew what had happened because his parents had carefully explained to him about how her heart wasn't working properly. He just didn't seem to be able to take it in. In the early days dealing with Matthew was not the main problem. The problem for me was coping with the comments of the other children who had not got the sensitivity to understand how Matthew was feeling. For example, Matthew might forget and say something like, 'My sister has a doll like that', only to be shouted down by a friend saying, 'You haven't got a sister, she's dead.' I probably was more aware of the pain these harsh words could cause. To Matthew it was a realisation that flowed into his thoughts in waves throughout the day. The death of his sister was just one facet of the change in his life. The other tragedy, which he was probably feeling more acutely, was the immense sorrow of his parents, which meant that his whole life had changed completely. He didn't know how to cope with their grief. His parents were different. Everything was different. The best way that I could help Matthew was to make the school experience as joyful as possible. The Bear was the answer. Matthew loved him. Each morning when he came into the classroom the first thing he did was give Bear a big hug. At first these were silent hugs, often repeated at intervals through the day. His thumb would find its way into his mouth and he would stay with the Bear for a prolonged hug. He was taking time out for comfort. He could have had a hug from me anytime he wanted, but hugs with a human usually involve words and he wasn't wanting explanations, just physical contact. Nor did he want to be the focus of attention for the other children, he needed to be comforted in an unobtrusive way. Children coming to terms with grief need someone or something to talk to who will just listen and remain silent. They just need to share their pain. We talk too much, we explain too much, we intrude too much. As time went on Matthew would talk to Bear about her and I would keep my distance, watch and eavesdrop. The first sign of total acceptance came when Bear settled into his hammock for his long sleep and Matthew brought one of his sister's teddies for Bear to cuddle, because she was dead and didn't need it any more. From then onwards he started to heal. We talked about her, she wasn't shut out of his life, but he could talk about her without outward sadness. His parents and the educational psychologist were very surprised that Matthew handled the situation so well. I think that our Bear played a crucial role in that healing process.

Emma

One morning Emma walked into the classroom, burst into tears and said that her Daddy was leaving and that she and her brother were going to stay with their mother. To make matters worse her father was going to work overseas and she wouldn't be able to see him again for a long time. Emma was completely devastated. For weeks she was on the verge of tears all the time, the slightest disagreement causing an hysterical outburst. This, quite understandably, alienated her from the other children in the class. At the age of six they did not have the level of understanding, or the tolerance to deal with such a fractious classmate. I gave her as much support as I could but in a busy classroom I wasn't always available for the prolonged cuddles which were really what she needed. Yet again, Bear filled the need. He became Emma's lunchtime partner and I made sure that she always had a space beside her so that Bear could sit and share her lunch. She poured all the pent-up emotion into caring for him and when they had finished eating they would sit together on the carpet and share a storybook and the much needed cuddle before she went out to play. Young children so desperately need physical contact as a form of comfort, but sadly in many cultures teachers are very wary of touching children for fear of accusations. When we bought our special 'reading chairs' for each classroom it was with the specific intention of sitting close to the child. How else can one feel the physical tension that a non-reader is experiencing, or be aware of the gradual relaxation as they make that transition into literacy? I found that I could predict to within a fortnight when a child would start to read independently just by sitting close and feeling the tension easing. I am digressing yet again, back to Emma. As with Matthew, the physical presence of the Bear and his ability to give unconditional loving response brought into the classroom the level of comfort that a child will find at home with a much loved cuddly toy. The main difference was that this was openly acceptable and not something restricted to bedtime comfort. Poor little Emma came to terms with the situation eventually, but the feeling of loss was ever present.

I have just concentrated on four children but could have gone on and on. Each child, in both classes, benefited in different ways and the Bear and the Little Witch gave them something to 'hang' the learning on, to enable deep learning to take place and to give comfort when needed.

Chapter 7

The whole curriculum

In many countries, a statutory subject-based curriculum for primary schools exists. The links that bind the strands of learning have been separated and have resulted in many schools adopting themes, in an attempt to contextualise the children's learning. In order that children will avoid repetition during their primary years, these themes tend to be fixed, so that, for example, all primary 1 children might be faced with a whole term of 'Myself and My Family' or 'Toys'. I can see the reasoning behind such a move, which encourages consistency across year bands and ensures that children don't spend their entire primary education drawing pictures of dinosaurs, but I found that my creativity was stifled by such an imposed restraint. I was happy to work with the curricular requirements, but the way I did it needed to inspire me, otherwise I could not pass enthusiasm on to the children.

Creating situations

What we need in classrooms, especially where there is a statutory curricular requirement, are catalysts that make enthusiastic learning possible. These don't have to be blanketing themes, but can be situations such as the one I stumbled across. I had never taught a full year with such an uninterrupted flow before, where the leads came naturally from the children and where year-round motivation was maintained by the children. In the past I had often dived enthusiastically into a new topic theme only to have it wend its way to a weary conclusion as the momentum was drowned by the need to complete the topic book. There were seldom endings that celebrated success, the end was usually a relief to everyone in the last minute flurry to complete the tasks and then breathe a big sigh of relief. Well, we never had that kind of pressure from our Bear and Little Witch, there was no 'topic book'. Instead the characters worked to pull the strands together, thus making the learning experiences whole for the children. At this point I will tease out and revisit certain learning areas to illustrate the argument and at the same time give more information about events mentioned earlier in the text.

Mathematics

We had spent more than a month working through the functional nature of the mathematics we were 'doing' every day. It was all a bit divorced from reality and was becoming rather dull and routine. Then, suddenly the investigation into the arrangements for the birthday party brought the whole subject alive. From the initial group work session when we discussed the menu for the picnic lunch, mathematical thinking came to the fore. Suddenly we had children pestering their parents to go to the supermarket so that they could research prices. It was the children who noticed that honey comes in jars in a range of sizes, which have a relationship to price. They also noticed that honey isn't just 'honey', there are different types. Honey is made from a variety of flower types, a tangent to pick up in another area of the curriculum, and the flower type also seemed to affect pricing. Apart from the mathematical implications we had very young children reading the labels on honey jars, eager to discover information, this was very pleasing. Here we were developing mathematics with a real purpose and reading because of an urgent need for information.

Bread was also a source of intense interest. Little fingers were hard at work counting the number of slices in packaged loaves. If everyone in the class, plus the invited guests had two large slices of bread each, how many loaves would we need? Then we got into discussion about different types of bread and comparative pricing.

Is brown bread better for us? Here was another tangent that took us into the cross-curricular realms of science and nutrition. The children found ways to get answers to their mathematical problems. Some used counting cubes to match people to pairs of sliced bread. Others worked it out with a series of addition sums. Some children went straight to the calculator and got an answer. At the end of the day we all sat down and compared results, talked about method, how had they arrived at their answer, how long had it taken, could they make a guess, an estimate before they started, to help them to know if their result was about right. We then added the result to the 'master' shopping list.

We would all need to have lots to drink, especially if there were going to be energetic games. How many bottles of drink would we have to buy? I can almost hear people saying let them drink water! I thought of that too, but my suggestion was met with total disdain. Nobody, but nobody drinks water at a birthday party, you have special drink, 'treat drink'! So, how were we going to work this one out? Simple, by using the water tray. As a teacher of young children I had used water play regularly. I knew all the reasons for doing it, concept formation being at the fore, but . . . whenever I saw young children standing around a water tray the overwhelming observation was that they were having a really good time playing. I don't for one minute want to suggest that they should be denied that pleasure or that they aren't learning at the same time. They are indeed learning a great deal, discovering how much water a variety of bottles, beakers and pots will hold, the power of water when it is moving very fast, and so on. I don't think though that they necessarily look closely at the capacity of the containers they are using or register that this is a litre and that one is 250ml. When they are sent to the water tray with a set of tasks to complete the compulsion to play often over-rides the requirement to complete the worksheet, or they get so wet that the facts on the paper are impossible to read when they return! In the situation of the birthday party we had a real purpose and a real problem to solve. So, armed with paper cups, of the birthday party variety, and a few empty economy-sized soft drink bottles with a litre capacity, they set off, in groups, to solve a real problem. How many paper cups of drink can we get from a litre bottle? Everyone had a go and they were even sensible with the paper that they recorded their results on. Again, we sat together as a class to compare results and then the really tricky task of calculating how many bottles we would need got under way. First we had to estimate how many drinks each person would need. It was agreed that four seemed about right. The number of 'drinkers' involved was large, so I suggested that they worked on groups of 10. How many bottles for 10 people? Again the children worked in groups and each group had to sort out how they were going to do it. There was one additional condition though and that was that they had to estimate first. There was no problem with this as it offered an extra challenge which children love. All the mathematics equipment was available for them to use. They had to make the selection. What often happens in infant classrooms is that teachers give the children the equipment they will need, it is usually all neatly laid out on the tables when the children come in. This makes for ease in classroom management but doesn't necessarily give the children the opportunity to make connections between task and tools. I'll never forget, with an earlier class of children of a similar age, telling them which equipment they should use only to be floored by one small boy who put his hand up and said, 'Mrs Tyrrell, can I just use my head?' One or two of them did just use their heads on this task and I was able to make a note of this observation.

Once all this information had been collected, and the master list completed, they then had to divide the cost by the number of children and round up to a sensible amount so that we wouldn't have a lot of small coins. Again, this did not prove to be a problem, they managed really well. Throughout this whole experience I was continually amazed by the ability of these six year olds when faced with a motivating challenge. By this time they were getting really good and so were ready for the final task. It had been agreed that we would all go to the local supermarket early on the morning of the party to buy everything. We had lots of mothers offering to help so that the children would be able to shop in groups of four. The real challenge was to sort out the shopping list so that every

Shopping for the party.

group had articles of a similar price to buy. Again, the children managed, it was like a big matching game.

A letter needed to be written to the parents telling them that no packed lunch would be needed that day and asking for the contribution towards the cost. Again, this was written, photocopied and distributed by the children.

On the day, we all set off really early, each group clutching their shopping list and the money in a purse. I had warned the supermarket that we were coming and everyone was really helpful. I think I mentioned in an earlier chapter that everything worked like clockwork with one group having the added pleasure of finding that peanut butter was on special offer, so they had cash in hand! (We later made a big wall display, with our shopping bags as the backing and put the shopping lists and lots of photos on it for everyone to see.) On our return we unpacked and the children started to prepare the picnic with the help of the mothers. The day was a great success due I think to the total ownership of the whole project by the children and the excitement of Bear's birthday. The party served another role for it was also an occasion to celebrate the successful outcome of a period of sustained hard work. We really do need to give children such opportunities. Standing in assembly holding their topic books isn't always enough.

Geography

I have a Canadian friend who laughs when I talk about my bear and she tells me that a bear is the very last thing you want in a Canadian classroom. In parts of Canada where she has worked bears are creatures to be feared and most definitely are not considered either cuddly or friendly. They even have 'Bear Alerts' when the children are not allowed out in the playground if there has been a bear sighting. However, for those in other parts of the world bears are acceptable companions. Where bears come from was obviously a natural focus for enquiry. The children collected all the books they could find about bears and then we found a big world map and located the countries where the different species live. Most of the bears came from cold climates, but one little boy, whose parents were from Burma, threw himself at me one morning and with great delight told me about the Sun Bear that is found in the forests of Burma. He was delighted and shared the information with everyone before writing about his discovery. Most of this writing was done in small books that our Bear would be able to read when all the children had gone home. Often the children would take their writing to the Bear first and read it to him before they showed it to me. This was good because young children seldom read back what they have written. As a result of all this research they built up a picture of the different climatic regions of the world and were able to make comparisons with the location of our school. Study of the different themes tended to be intense bursts of interest, when we would spend big chunks of the day focusing on these leads. They always involved literacy activities with frequent sessions around the easel, and lots of purposeful reading and writing. This was the way our days went. I had an overall plan of the integration of subjects but was also open to the directions that took the interest of the children. The whole hibernation situation came about as a result of the children's investigations and their desire to do what was right for their bear. It wasn't something that I had anticipated but was important, so my plans needed to change. We were led on a 'need to know' basis and my role was very much to help the children to learn and to lead them to the resources that help to make learning possible, rather than an information giver who stopped the learning that was going on and changed tack at hourly intervals. My planning therefore wasn't a straitjacket, I planned for the skills I wanted the children to acquire rather than the specific content knowledge.

It all worked so well, it just rolled along. One day I woke with a high fever and had to phone the Deputy Head to ask her to find supply cover. Her immediate reaction was to say, 'No Jenny, we'll sit the Bear in the "reading chair" and he can be in charge.' It might sound silly to say it, but actually that might have worked! I never did find out what the supply teacher thought about it all.

Science

Bear had a very special role in all learning experiences and as I come to each subject area and think about his influence, memories leap out at me. As a result of the birthday party and the discussions about food, we were led into talking about nutrition, which led on to work on dental care. We actually made a huge set of teeth with decay and plaque, fillings and loose teeth, which we had to step through to get from one side of the room to the other. That was such fun.

Our work on light is an area that I would like to focus upon.

When introducing any new material to young children we need to find something that will spark their interest. We can't just sit six-year-old children down and say, 'Right, today we are going to talk about light', can we? That I suppose is the traditional way to do it. There has to be a way to make the children feel that the need to learn new things is urgent and that it comes from them. My husband is an architect and I'll never forget him saying, in a very whimsical way, that the key to success with clients was to sow the seeds of ideas and then let them think that they had thought of the solution all by themselves. We should be using the same techniques with young children.

We were going to absorb this new knowledge about light into our learning around February, when it just so happens that the sun's rays in the northern hemisphere are very low. I have one or two crystals at home and I brought them in and put them on the sill of a high window. As the afternoon sunlight filtered in we suddenly had rainbow patterns all over the classroom. The children were spellbound because it was such a beautiful sight. They started looking around to see why it had happened. It wasn't raining and sunny at the same time, so the usual cause of rainbows in the sky didn't apply. Then someone noticed my crystal. I took it down and the rainbows disappeared. There were shrieks of horror, so I put it back and we enjoyed the light show for the next hour or so. I didn't suddenly launch into a scientific explanation, I didn't whisk out the next topic book. We just enjoyed the experience and I left them to think about it.

The next day, surprise, surprise two or three children came to school with crystals carefully wrapped in their school bags. Lots of the children had been talking about our rainbows at home and were eager to share what their Mum or Dad had said. There was a natural lead into the obvious statement, 'Let's find out about it.' Sutton-Smith (1988) writes: 'Every subject matter requires its own "what if" speculation, its own place in the imagination.' Well, the 'what ifs' had certainly fired the imaginations of these children. That afternoon we set the crystals on the window sill again, but we were out of luck because the sun was not on cue, it was a really cloudy afternoon. We were all very annoyed. However, the next day we had outstanding success and had rainbows going every-where. By opening the classroom door we even managed to have one shining on the corridor so that people passing by could share in the fun. The children also made sure that we had a big rainbow shining on our hibernating Bear. By this time they were getting impatient for him to wake up and thought that might do the trick.

The obvious result of all of this interest was that we moved into a short, all embracing period when we looked at light. The children had so many questions that needed answering and I had to be ten steps ahead in my own knowledge! Again, we made some lovely books. . . . And Bear's influence? Well, he was the vehicle for the writing. They were worried that when he woke up he would be really behind in his learning, because he had missed so much, so they made books for him to read as soon as he woke. There was no need for attainment tests, the data was all there, collected in a natural, formative way. Years later the children still had very clear memories of the way we split the sunlight to give us the different colours of the spectrum.

Art and Design and Technology

As with all subject areas the work evolved naturally and flowed from one project to the next. Whilst 'light' was illuminating our learning we made a big rainbow, which arched across the class-room. The children experimented with colours and watched as red and yellow made orange and yellow and blue made green, making the connections with the colours in our big rainbow. Whatever we were doing, the artistic potential was exploited and the results were recycled from classroom to corridor so that the children's efforts could be shared. I tried to add explanation wherever possible so that staff and parents could have made explicit the educational value of what we were doing. Creating bright colourful environ-ments for children to learn in has far more to it than interior design.

With their learning displayed all around them, the children who needed more time to absorb new knowledge had a chance to make the connections that others made more quickly. In the case of the autistic child, it was the way she learned best and was therefore

'High-bear-nating'.

crucial to her progress. Again I feel that children also need to know about these issues, it's good for them to realise that we are not just making the classroom look pretty but that the displays are helping them to learn. The obvious next step is that it gives the children involvement in the decision to take down displays when the learning is complete.

Our project to create a hammock for the hibernation was the result of a great deal of thought as we puzzled over where the Bear could sleep in our crowded classroom. Again, we were working with a real situation that needed to be solved, we weren't dealing with an abstract concept, which young children find harder to absorb and relate to. They were certainly smart enough to know that we needed help and a Cub Pack leader was the person to target for assistance. Bear's height and width were measured so that he would have a made-to-measure hammock. A lot of discussion went into the type of string we should use, no one wanted Bear to fall out because it wasn't strong enough to hold him. So we collected many samples and chose the strongest twine, which happened to be a nice bright colour. We looked for pictures of hammocks to choose a design and discovered that we would need two pieces of wood at either end. Eventually, with the help of our 'scouting' expert the plaiting began with bright red cord around a broomstick, which had been cut in half. Large cup hooks were screwed into the pin board frames and amidst great excitement the hammock was put into place in a corner of the classroom. Again, we had an occasion to celebrate a job well done.

Music

Our school was fortunate to have a talented music teacher. Wherever possible she attempted to link her teaching to what was happening in the children's classrooms. She was a true ally in the fun of these fantasy figures. Occasionally, if he promised to be very good, Bear would go to the music room to join in the lesson. It was always a joyful event because Linda entered fully into the spirit of the situation. She found lots of songs about bears for the children to learn and we wrote the words into a book. There seem to be very strong links between music and early literacy acquisition. The child knows the song by heart and can follow the words, maintaining the fluency supplied by the tune and matching the sung words to the marks on the page. In a way it's a natural form of rote learning that has such emphasis in eastern cultures. Also, children love songs and so get repeated practice that is natural and pleasurable. Songbooks were always a popular choice for private reading and I made sure that we also had the words of the current songs clearly displayed around the classroom. There was also an added benefit in that there was another teacher involved in what I was doing whom I could bounce ideas off and also get ideas from. Linda would often ask the children for the latest classroom happenings with both classes and they delighted in keeping her up to date. There was a sharing of the pleasure of it all.

The links between the work in the classroom and the focus of specialist staff's teaching all helped to give consistency and continuity to the children's learning experience. The catalyst for this was the fantasy figures. The influence of our extra classmate therefore permeated through every aspect of the school day and motivated, sustained and strengthened the children's learning.

Chapter 8

'He was real on the inside'

Here, the children's voices are heard, as they recollect memories after two years and after four years. It was so interesting to have the opportunity to sit down with a group of children and reminisce about the learning in which we were all involved. This was something that I had never experienced before, other than conversations with past pupils in the playground. I found that I was a bit nervous, as we don't usually ask such young learners to evaluate our teaching. I think that we should consider doing it from time to time.

What came through in all the early interviews with the children was the social element of Bear and Little Big Feet's presence in the classroom, 'and when you were lonely you had someone to play with,' or words to that effect, appeared again and again. I was disturbed to discover that there was such depth of loneliness within a small classroom filled with lively six year olds. Do children have a sense of isolation in a crowd? Throughout this book I seem to be raising questions and not necessarily supplying answers. I suppose this is why I feel compelled to write about these special experiences, in the hope that someone reading my reflections will be fired to follow a tentative lead.

Memories of the Bear

> Bear used to help us to be more generous and kind to other people.

Talking with the children two, three, four years afterwards raised all sorts of extra benefits that I had not really noticed. The opening statement was true, it was a very peaceful year, lacking the conflicts one is normally used to dealing with on a daily basis, the children were definitely happier. I was also constantly amazed at the depth of their perception, for they knew it was special and rather strange too. One child said; 'I told him when my Grandad died of a heart attack and Bear ended up crying with me.'

Another priceless response to my question, 'What was it like having Bear in the classroom?' was, 'He was just like Jesus Christ, sort of kind.'

The Bear group, understandably, mentioned his influence on their reading and writing far more than the second class with the witch. One boy said that Bear liked to listen to the 'Lego' books, which we made in the class. After a minute he smiled and said; 'They were the books that I could read best, weren't they, Mrs Tyrrell?'

The 'Lego' books evolved from a need to have material that the boys were really interested in. They collected pictures from catalogues and I added a simple text, sometimes in rhyming couplets when I felt inspired, more often than not they were descriptions of how to make something. They were very popular and at one point I had my eye on the big educational catalogues in the staffroom, but we didn't have old copies and I lacked the courage to attack the current editions with a pair of scissors. It would be a good thing to do though.

As the children grew older and further removed from the experience, they were able to be even more analytical. Another boy remembered reading, *We're Going on a Bear Hunt*. He said;

> Bear's best story was the Bear Hunt, when the children came to the cave they ran all the way home, through the grass and the mud and the river and the forest. I used to read that to him over and over, that was because I could read it wasn't it.

Another remembered that: 'he liked to read stories about himself and all the stories we wrote about the Wild Things'. At the time I obviously wasn't aware of just how significant he was as an audience for their own written work, otherwise I would have exploited the situation more. I knew he was invaluable as a listener to the published texts which they read to him, but of course he was also enjoying their own stories in his normal unthreatening, uncritical way.

They all had very clear memories of the research work we did with reference books. One child recounted that:

> We all went to get the books, then we looked for 'B', we saw 'Banana', so we looked on and when we got to 'Bear' we stopped and read. Then we made a big chart with everything on it.

John, who caused me the greatest concern as a reader, shared this conversation with one of his friends about the little girl who would not speak:

J. I didn't read to him much, well I pretended to, but I think Joanna did.

M. She did, but that's because she didn't speak much to us.

J. Yes, that was very strange.

M. She still speaks quietly now, but she does speak to us.

J. A bit more, she's a bit louder, getting a bit louder. Yeh.

They cared about Joanna, they were aware that there was something wrong, but they were always gentle with her. John became a reader very slowly. No doubt the 'pretending to' was a helpful stage in the process. By the end of his primary 2 year he could read known texts with confidence. It was another year before he could tackle an unknown text. He made it, very slowly. He had retained his pleasure in books, which was a blessing and had a self-esteem a little bruised but not deeply scarred.

They all talked at length about Bear's appalling spelling.

He wasn't a very good speller, but he was quite good at the easy words like 'I' and 'the', you know. Do you remember when we taught him about 'tion' words?

I remember well, there was some problem we were trying to resolve and Bear wrote them a message one night, which began:

I fink Iv got a slooshun.

They loved his messages and took enormous delight in trying to make sense of his emergent writing. Someone suggested that we should make a big 'word list' of the 'tion' pattern for him. Over the next three or four days they collected over thirty words which end with 'tion'. Of course, we sat Bear in the chair and read the words to him and Bear responded well to their teaching and started to use the correct form. This was really exciting because they were all able to learn in a totally unthreatening way, from his mistakes. We did this often, not so often that it became common-place for then the children would have smelled a rat and realised that the situation was contrived. Some of Bear's messages in the early days of his time with us were so obscure that it would take a couple of hours to decipher them. I would leave the paper on the easel and the children would wander over and puzzle over it until someone eventually shouted 'I've got it,' then we would stop what we were doing and have a look. I did so much direct teaching, to a totally focused class with scrappy bits of paper and strange scribbled messages. Again, the motivation was fun, it was all such fun. Laughter is such an important aid to teaching, creating a feel good factor, which seems to make the learning easier. There is plenty of research now about the healing effects of laughter and many hospitals around the world have 'clown doctors' to make seriously sick children laugh. There seem to be links with all sorts of quick recoveries, so why not with the stresses of learning?

They all remembered the stories they wrote. Andrew, whose writing progress I chronicled in the chapter on writing said; 'I wrote and drew about multi-coloured bears with big tummy buttons.' Then he collapsed into giggles. These were happy memories of what, at the time, had been quite a struggle.

Four years after the Bear year, just before they left the school to go to secondary schools, they still had very vivid memories. A group of four boys reminisced thus in a piece of shared writing.

> Bear was our cuddly friend hibernating in his hammock in the corner. He woke up because he smelt the cake. We also read lots of books with him. Once we even had a catastrophe or a 'bearastrophe' when we couldn't decide which loo Bear should go in, the girls or the boys. Then some visitors came along and stared at us because all the girls were in the boys loo having a look and the boys were in the girls.
>
> It was great fun when the whole class and Bear tried to squeeze under your huge umbrella and we succeeded.
>
> When we turned off the lights and closed all the windows the light beams from the sunlight made the crystal shine and we had rainbows.
>
> The class photo was fun when Bear joined in. We have lots of happy memories.

I asked some of these eleven year olds whether they even thought about him not being real. One boy thought for a few minutes and then found the words to describe how he felt, 'Well, he was real on the inside.' Yes, that's what it was. At the time of this conversation, a big eleven-year-old lad wrapped his arms around himself in a kind of hug and said, 'It gives me a lovely warm feeling just remembering.' That was good, a very good day.

Memories of Little Big Feet

I have decided to include three complete interviews here. When I conducted these interviews, again two years after the event, I remembered an article in which Labov suggested that interviewers should address the socio-linguistic factors which control speech by making the interview situation as informal as possible. So I took along potato chips and talked to the children in twos. This resulted in a striking difference in the volume of speech, but it wasn't easy to transcribe amidst the munching and the crackle of crisp packets! I suppose that now I would be better taking apples or carrots, I apologise to those deeply concerned about health matters.

I use the child's initial rather than name and refer to myself as T.

Interview I

T. What can you remember about LBF in our classroom?

D. I thought it was nice when she locked us out. She was being naughty and she was knocking all the toys off the shelves and I thought it was fun when we cleared up.

T. You didn't mind clearing up when she made the mess?

D. Uh-huh.

S. I liked it when she put the carpet on my bed and I couldn't pull the sheet up.

T. . . . when she was at your house? What else did she do when she went home?

D. I had this little tree in a pot that had mandarins on it, and when I woke up all the mandarins were on the floor and the tree was bare.

T. What about your Grandad's birthday cake?

D. Oh, yes, that was a funny one. When I woke up, um, I couldn't find her, I forgot that maybe yesterday I took her back because I forgot, and um, when I got the milk for my breakfast I saw that part of my Grandad's cake was eaten and there was a big hole in the middle and she was sitting on top of it.

T. We have a lovely photo of the witch in the fridge. Did either of you ever read her stories?

D. I read to her at home before I went to bed.

T. What sort of stories did she like?

D. There's this story called *Bears in the Night*, where they all got out of bed and walked all around, and there was this spooky hill and they all ran back down. She liked that.

T. She probably enjoyed spooky things.

D. Yes, it was at night and it was spook hill, but it wasn't really scary, it was just an owl going hoo-hooo, and they were scared of it.

T. Did you ever read to her, Susannah?

S. I forgot.

T. Do you think she helped you learn to write?

D. Well, I think she helped me, um, remember to do little letters instead of capitals, she had to remember 'cos she's got capital letters in her name.

S. Mrs Tyrrell, have you got some more ink for Mr Pen?

D. I think he's dead.

T. No he's not, he's around somewhere. I'll get some more ink and when I come back I'll use him with another class.

T. Did you ever tell her secrets?

D. I told her secrets but I forget what. I remember one time when I took her home she sat on my clock, my grandfather clock, and it stopped at midnight. When we woke up I looked at the clock and I said, 'Hey, Mummy, look it's midnight, let's go back to bed?'

T. . . . and what did Mummy say?

D. Mummy said, 'It's light, it's morning the clock must be wrong, or you can't tell the time,' and she looked at the clock and she saw LBF holding the toothbrush and the toothbrush was pointing to the twelve.

S. Maybe it was twelve o'clock at lunch time.

D. She wanted it to be. My Mum said something happens at midnight.

T. That's right, some people call it the witching hour.

D. Yer, the witching hour.

T. She had terrible teeth didn't she, do you remember?

S. Yes, they were all yellow and purple too. We had to teach her how to clean them, but she kept losing her toothbrush because she used it to fly on, like a broomstick.

D. When she went to my house, when I put her in bed with me, when I woke up she had a new toothbrush in her hand, one of mine . . . and I looked in the bin and I saw a broken one. She must have broken hers because she didn't like it so she used mine.

It was all such fun.

S. She liked green toothbrushes, everybody kept giving her green toothbrushes.
D. I had a green toothbrush and she grabbed it because the other one was blue or red.
S. Where is she now?
T. I took her to school with me, I'll bring her back, I promise.

My initial reaction to this interview was the awareness that one child was dominating the discussion, but that was to be expected really. Douglas was very outgoing with a wonderfully developed imagination while Susannah was a more thoughtful child, often providing the starting points for Douglas to expand. It was interesting that they both thought it was fun clearing up the mess that LBF made, a technique to be noted!

When Douglas was talking about the capital letters, Susannah mentioned Mr Pen. Mr Pen to me was a very, very incidental character but was obviously very important to the children.

Interview 2

This took place on the same day, with the same accompanying munching noises.

T.   What can you remember about LBF in our classroom?

L.   I went to Catherine's house when Catherine had LBF and she put on my ballet shoes and Catherine's cup cake dress and hat and in the morning she looked real funny.

T.   Weren't the shoes a bit big for her?

L.   Yes, about the size of her body.

C.   I remember the morning she locked us out of the classroom.

T.   What did we find when we got into the classroom?

C.   A big, big mess. There were crumbs on the carpet and the Lego was tipped out.

L.   . . . and she was hanging by her toes on the line!

T.   What did she look like?

L.   She had green hair, and it was nearly falling off, she . . . she would have been bald if it did.

C.   She had a winter uniform,

L.   . . . that was made for her,

C.   . . . and when she came home with me she fell in the bath and her real clothes got spoiled so she had a special school uniform.

T.   How did she travel?

C.   On her broomstick, which was a toothbrush.

L.   When she got to my house I put her in the store room, I got a piece of toast and I put peanut butter on it because I thought she'd be like me and like it. She didn't like it though and it was dribbling out of her mouth.

T.   Did you ever read stories to her?

C. Yes.
L. I didn't but I took pictures of her.
C. She liked to hear my bedtime stories.
T. We wrote our own stories about her, didn't we?
L. On my writing about her, it went in the magazine. It said that I took her to ballet and I put her on the wooden steps and she moved to the black chair. She watched us dancing on the stage.
T. You used to write lots of stories yourself, didn't you?
L. Yes I did. I still do, I've got a big book that I've got to finish by tomorrow. It's got twenty-six pages in it and I've got to finish it for my writer's badge at Brownies because I love writing.
T. Do you think she helped us with our learning?
C. No, she was awful at everything.
L. She did. She helped us with our writing because we wrote about her and she had to sit there and pose.
T. Did you ever share secrets with her?
L. I did but I can't tell because you'll tell someone. Why didn't you bring her to see us?
T. I'm sorry, I left her at home.
L. Well, who's looking after her then?
T. My family, I'll promise to bring her another time.
L. I'll always remember her. We've got nothing now, but I've got the magazine to look at to remind me.

Again, in this interview one child tended to dominate, but there was far more shared remembering early on. 'She helped us with our writing because she had to sit there and pose.' What a poignant statement. The content of Lisa's writing was outstanding, some of her stories were good enough for professional publication. Here she was, a very young child still, likening the witch's role in the writing process to an artist with a model. She really cared about that little witch and became quite aggressive in her questioning of me towards the end. The final comment was sad, two years later she still missed the little witch. I suppose that the children developed the same kind of relationship with these characters as they do with a favourite cuddly toy that goes right through life, there is a special bond. Perhaps what I had created were classroom 'comforters'.

Interview 3

T. What was the most special thing about having the witch in the classroom?

C. Taking her home. Well, when I took her home we have these little books called *Peter Rabbit* and *Tom Kitten* and when I woke up in the morning she was sitting on my bed reading them.

T. What happened at your house, Patricia?

P. Well, the first time I took her home something really naughty happened. We, we had this mirror, right, it was in the bathroom and when we were making the barbecue the little witch went upstairs, took my Mummy's best lipstick down and wrote 'I love it here' on the mirror and my Mummy said, 'Patricia, did you do that?' and I didn't it was the little witch.

T. Did she spoil Mummy's lipstick?

P. She actually broke it in half.

T. Can you remember any of the things she used to do in the classroom?

C. When she made that big mess in the classroom and she locked us out.

P. Well, we had to clear up the big mess.

C. She left us to tidy it up.

P. And she muddled up all the aprons. Anyway, she would have said she hadn't done it.

C. But Mr Pen would have seen. Once when I was riding my bike she wanted to come with me so I put her in my basket.

T. We wrote stories about her.

C. I've still got them. One story was about when she came to my house.

P. I've got that one too.

T. Do you think she helped us with our learning?

C. No, not exactly, but Mr Pen helped us.

P.   He taught us joined up writing and how to do 'O's properly.

C.   And she had horrid teeth, they were all yellow.

P.   . . . and purple.

C.   . . . because she ate too many biscuits, because when she made the mess she tipped all the biscuits out and she probably ate lots.

P.   We learned about teeth and how we didn't have any when we were babies, and how to look after them.

T.   Where did she come from?

C.   Um, yes, the book.

P.   I was the first to see her. She was hanging on the picture line, upside down.

C.   Yes, and then one day she was hanging upside down among the numbers.

P.   . . . with all the witches on, the very odd witches and the even ones.

T.   Was it special having her in the class?

P.   Oh yes.

C.   But I want her to come back.

Patricia's mother was responsible for the message on the mirror, and for breaking her own lipstick. Shared fantasy experiences can be very meaningful. When these experiences are shared between home and school then they seem to hold even more appeal for the children. I found it interesting that the children saw Mr Pen as the figure who helped their learning. He, of course, had an instructional role, which more resembled the stereotype of the teacher. It is intriguing that even at this young age children see teachers as instructors. When I have asked children if their parents ever teach them anything at home, the response is usually 'no'. When pressed to explain how they learned to eat properly, or ride a bike they would respond that their Mum or Dad 'showed' them how to do it, or 'did it with them'. The verb 'to teach' is kept for institutional learning.

I was also pleased that Patricia remembered the odd and even numbers. We had painted some very odd witches for the odd numbers and made symmetrically correct witches for the evens. These were then hung on a 'washing line' across the room so that they were always there for reference.

I wonder whether they would have had such vivid memories without LBF. I don't think so. In another interview I asked a child what special memories he had of his primary 1 year. He thought for a long time and eventually said, 'I could run faster than Tom.' That was all he could remember. He couldn't remember anything the class had done, but I am sure that there were high spots.

What I think was happening was that these children had something to 'hang' their learning onto. This of course is one of the major arguments in favour of topic work and thematic learning, but I feel that the fantasy element took this a step further because the learning was embedded in shared fun. I remember as a child being enthralled when my mother's large family got together and the stories would start. Someone would say, 'Do you remember when . . .'. And the story would unravel. It was always something amusing and that would trigger other memories. It can be the same with young children's learning.

Chapter 9

Implications for practice

> Intellectual skills when not enlivened by imagination, lack the ingredient that makes them educationally alive.
>
> (Kieran Egan, 1992)

So here I am, nearly at the end of this journey of reflection, facing the task of pulling together all the experiences, thoughts, unanswered questions and suggestions in order to make sense of what happened. I began this finale with a quote from the work of Kieran Egan. His writing has enlightened my thinking and been a great resource to arm my intellect and strengthen my conviction when I have had to justify my seemingly strange ideas. I recommend his works to anyone interested in further reading.

I will begin this conclusion by going back to the beginning and looking at the qualities young children bring with them when they start school. The question I pose is, do we build on the firm base of pre-school learning or create new foundations that better suit the curriculum?

What does the young child bring to school?

Apart from a school bag containing his lunch and 'reading book', the young child brings a vast store of knowledge about learning. He has mastered the ability to communicate in at least one language. He has a firm knowledge about his home environment and the position he holds within his family structure. He is likely to be a competent user of modern technology and will be able to operate the television, radio, CD player, video recorder, and computer as a source of enjoyment and information. He has acquired learning skills on a 'need to know' basis rather than 'you must learn'. He has also developed a strong intellectual capacity for imaginative thinking, which is very easily observed when watching any pre-school child at play. He has developed all sorts of strategies for remembering useful facts and he knows a great deal about feelings and emotions, for they control his primary needs.

This knowledge of emotions was the essence of Sylvia Ashton Warner's work with her Maori children in New Zealand. Strong emotions fired their motivation to write. The love my children felt for the Bear and the Little Witch ignited their ability to learn in similar ways. They learnt quickly and thoroughly because they were emotionally involved with the learning.

Another feeling that is a reality for most children in the world is being cared for. They in turn need to care for others, hence the dolls, cuddly toys and imaginary friends that are permanent features of those early years. I still have my toy rabbit, wrapped in plastic, because he is falling apart. I couldn't possibly throw him away because he is part of me and who I am. The Bear and Little Witch answered those deep needs too, but in a social, collective, rather than individual way. When Matthew needed comfort, Bear was always there at school, whilst his own favourite toy was safe at home. The figures gave the children additional emotional support in an environment that contained the stresses of formal learning.

The children also had emotionally enriching private conversations with the Bear. They all talked to him, but some more than others. For small children, talking to a toy is a kind of halfway point in expressing inner feelings. They are not quite ready to share with someone who will give a response and question their reasoning, so they go to a listener who will not voice an opinion. It's a bit like a baby talking to herself in her cot before she falls asleep.

Enjoying the sound of self-initiated utterance and practising the sounds she hears spoken to her. My children's conversations with the Bear gave them the chance to practise stress and intonation whilst they acted out a social interaction. It also gave them an opportunity to talk openly in complete trust, in a way serving a similar function to a confessor. It was totally private and would never be repeated. When they read a story to the Bear there was that same element of safety and trust. Bear would not correct or scold. He gave them the opportunity for extended, stress free practice.

The child also brings with him a deep knowledge of how spoken language works. The fact that the children wrote to the Bear and Little Witch meant that they were able to use that already acquired knowledge and use the genre with which they were most familiar. As I have mentioned earlier, this was a key to the children's success in writing. They also wrote a great deal and had a lot of direct teaching, but I think that the written conversations were the most important factor.

There is one other reflection that might make some readers throw their arms up in horror. I think that moments with the Bear gave children space, time out from the need to be continually 'on task'. 'Keep the children on task' has been the battle cry of the last decade, 'give them some space to think and absorb' would be a good replacement for the next. My best thinking time for this piece of writing has been whilst I have been out walking. Whenever I've got stuck I've gone for a walk, miles and miles and miles! If we want children to do a special piece of writing we should perhaps tell them about it the day before. Not indulge in a quick bit of motivation and give them thirty minutes to complete the 'task'. Young children need to play out new experiences. They need time to practise and sort things out perhaps to talk things over at home as they did with the rainbows.

Parental involvement

The involvement of the parents in the learning of their children during these two years was special. One mother said that all she had to say to her daughter was, 'What's the Bear been doing today?' and information poured out. No longer the, 'Oh, nothing much,' response, but a detailed account of what we had been doing. I suppose it was just sharing the fun of the day to the child, but it had a reassuring effect on the parents who didn't need to worry about their child's progress. This then had a snowball effect; because the parents were not anxious they did not put pressure on their children, life was happier at home and so the children thrived at school. When parent interviews came round we seemed to spend most of our time talking about those extra members of the class. The 'Bear' parents were eager to meet him and the 'Little Witch' parents would come in talking about the naughty things she had done on her visits to their homes. I would have totally bizarre conversations with parents who were obviously 'in the fantasy', or maybe it was that they thought I was! I suppose we all were and that was an important point for the well-being of the children. After a while, I realised that the parents were thoroughly enjoying the fun of it all too. We were in an 'everyone wins' situation. In quite a lengthy career I have never had such supportive groups of parents working with me. There seemed to be a stronger, more trusting partnership.

Many of the parents noticed the speed of their children's progress and soon made the connection with the fantasy element in the classroom. Especially with the Little Witch group where there was a requirement that the children would write about her visits home. Now children were writing at home with their parents from choice, there was no nagging or cajoling. The children wanted their writing to be neat so they practised at home before their turn came. Notes, letters and cards were also scribbled to the Bear and brought to school, the children wrote and wrote and wrote.

Attendance

I seemed to have a slight problem with the school secretary and the volunteer mothers who ran our medical room. It would appear that my class had the highest 'sent home because sick' rating. When I compared this with the attendance register it was clear that we had a higher than usual percentage of full attendance. What was happening was that the children were refusing to stay at home if they were sick, or they didn't tell their Mum if they felt unwell in the morning, because they didn't want to miss anything at school. It got to be a bit of an embarrassment that my children were the only ones being sent home with fevers and spots. Again, everything had a knock-on effect, they were happy and motivated, had regular attendance and obviously their learning benefited. Egan (1992) quotes Comenius who said; 'that if we arranged learning properly, children would come to school with as much joy as they go to the fair'. Our learning was indeed joyful.

The socialising element of schooling

Would it not be wonderful if the sole purpose of schooling was to open up the world of learning to all children in a natural, joyful way. Unfortunately that is not so, for a great deal of our time is spent regimenting children into 'schoolish' behaviour. I remember earlier I mentioned my son putting his hand up at the dinner table at home, seeking permission to speak. It was initially funny, but contained an underlying sadness. He was being conditioned, institutionalised. The Bear and Little Witch years made me question deeply what I was doing and what we as a profession do to children in the name of education. I got into trouble from time to time, and the thing that seemed to give most affront to the administrators of the school, was my flagrant disobedience about the way I greeted my class in the playground each morning. The rule was that when the bell rang the children were to line up in silence and were not supposed to speak again until they were all inside their classrooms. I managed to conform in previous years, but the very special relationship I had with these children meant that I really, really needed to go along the line each morning and say a special hello to everyone. It didn't take long, most children only needed a cheery greeting, but some of them needed to say something special or have a chance to restart the day if leaving home had been fraught with problems. They were all individuals and needed more than 'hello everyone' when they were quietly seated cross-legged on the classroom carpet. Or worse still as the teacher calls the

register and the greeting is so public th...
response than 'Yes Miss.' That's not wh...
are six years old. You say hello when y...
school, it would seem natural instincts have...
children have to conform to rules and regulation...
children need to move quietly about the school...
for the sake of safety, and I was quite happy to...
in silence if need be. While I am on the subject...
what sterile places most of them are for children...
Children need places to hide ... the kind of env...
allows imaginative play to blossom. Not all children...
about or kick a ball around. In this modern world wh...
have little chance to play out after school in large gr...
me to use the word gangs but that is what I really mean...
school playgrounds should allow them to play creatively i...
What I think these two years gave the children was this...
opportunity, but inside the classroom. We were all involv...
all encompassing fantasy game that went on all ye... It was...
gentle, comforting, exciting, entertaining, and motivating t...
as being a catalyst for learning.

Curriculum and teacher autonomy

My relationship with the curriculum was not a problem at all
during those years. I seemed to have no difficulty at all absorbing
the requirements into my planning. All I needed was a bit of time
to come up with an idea to sow the seeds of enquiry in the children's minds. The problem I did have was in being a member of a
three-teacher 'year band team'. All these teams within the whole
school were supposed to sit down together and plan the programme for each term. This is the sort of planning that gives rise
to ninety identical sunflowers on individual pieces of card deco-
rating the corridors of infant schools in early autumn, the only
differentiation being the name in the bottom right-hand corner. I
wouldn't mind so much if they were all cut out and made into a
field of sunflowers. It would be even better if there was an element
of design technology, so that the flower heads could turn towards

the sun. I just could not conform to this pattern. I was happy to discuss the subject content to be covered and the skills we would work on, but the way I did it and how I introduced the concepts to the children needed to spring from my own imagination on a daily and weekly basis. I couldn't possibly sit down one afternoon in late August and plan for a group of children I hadn't begun to work with yet, to the level of detail that had become the norm. The group planning in some cases even led to decisions for class outings. Now, my idea of total horror is the thought of an outing with ninety plus children, never mind how many adults are present. Just imagine having taken ninety on my supermarket trip!

I can see all the arguments for consistency of approach across year bands, and consistency in the way reading and writing are taught, mathematical terminology is used, etc. but I have a sneaking feeling that instead of the children it is the teachers who probably benefit most from this sort of conveyor belt planning. Why? Because they are cutting down on individual planning and take a comforting group decision on what is to be done. It makes one safe from individual criticism. The danger is that it can in some cases endorse mediocrity. Egan (1992) says that.

> Teachers in an educational system that takes imagination seriously must, then, be accorded a greater degree of autonomy. They cannot be treated as consumers and distributors of the contents of curriculum guides, nor as animated textbooks, nor as worksheet pedlars.

In some educational cultures, where primary schools work with subject specialists as in secondary establishments, then this practice is fine because it usually fits into a textbook-bound curriculum anyway.

Another issue raised by these two years is that of topic integration. For the first time in many years I did not have a topic as the linking agent for all the learning but a situation instead. I have a feeling that many children are almost themed out! I well remember hearing a child complain that they 'even had to sing songs about seasons and it was all getting so boring'. If variety is the spice of life, then maybe there is a possibility that some children find topics a bit constricting and all they remember is that they were 'doing seasons', but not what they did.

Memory

Many of the parents have said that their children have retained most of the details of the learning during those years. It was as though they had such happy memories to hang the learning on and the Bear and the Little Witch fixed the learning in deep memory. Even four years later I was amazed at the things the children remembered that I had long forgotten. Much of the knowledge they retained because of a need to tell Bear after his hibernation. This was another key to the successful outcome. There was truly purposeful learning taking place. The right sort of purpose that is, that did not involve learning in order to regurgitate the information for a test or examination. That sort of learning is soon forgotten.

Deepening thinking skills

Without doubt the situational learning that took place in those two years had a great influence on the systematic development of the children's thinking skills. They were constantly facing challenges and seeking solutions. The problems were real to the children and therefore were entered into whole-heartedly. You only have to think back to the birthday party to see the effect the Bear had on their application of mathematics to fully appreciate the difference.

Very young children rarely have real challenges to face in their school learning and yet they are probably at the stage when their ability to make sense of the world is most finely tuned. They can be persistent focused learners when the outcome is something they really want.

They also developed very good collaborative skills for working in small groups. They became so used to working in this way that colleagues came to expect to walk past my room and see children sprawled across tables intent on jotting ideas onto big sheets of paper. Their ideas were our starting point. My role was to help them refine them when we came together as a class.

When we put together the very hurried assembly I was staggered by their ability and it really brought home to me the fact that we so often underestimate these young learners.

Throughout both years the children were challenged day after day and each time they astounded me. So, of course, their learning accelerated because their cognitive ability was stimulated. Again, I quote Egan (1992):

> To be imaginative, then, is not to have a particular function highly developed, but it is to have heightened capacity in all mental functions. It is not, in particular something distinct from reason, but rather it is what gives reason flexibility, energy and vividness. It makes all mental life more meaningful, it makes life more abundant.

Continuity

So many important features of this whole experience were stumbled upon almost accidentally. When we were reaching the end of the Bear year and the children had negotiated with their next teacher that he could go with them, the very best element of continuity emerged, via the children. They worried that Bear's standard was way behind all of them and they hit upon the idea that they could take lots of things from my classroom to the next. So they made a list of books, which Bear could read, which meant that there would also be books there that they could read with confidence and pleasure. Then there were all our letter pattern lists that had been such a valuable resource. Of course they had to go too. Why, oh why, had I not thought of doing this before? Perhaps because in this special circumstance with the Bear he made it possible. There again was a reason for the suggestion. If I had offered my well-worn letter pattern sheet in previous years the next teacher would probably have turned her nose up in disgust. For the continuity of the children's learning it was important that they had all their familiar learning props, which they were used to handling, otherwise learning tends to stop during the period of readjustment. They also had a large, brown, cuddly link with the familiar on that first day back after the long summer holidays.

Fun

I have gone through all the expected implications and now arrive at what I see as really the most important feature when thinking about the education of young children, fun. We had fun, oh so much fun. Laughter was a very real part of every day. School can be a very serious place and the beneficial effect of laughter is now well documented. The children were relaxed, happy and secure so of course they learned. The sort of playing they do naturally at home was brought into the classroom. I firmly believe that we should build on those life experiences that children bring with them and adapt them into formal learning.

For those two classes of children and me, their teacher, 'fancy' did not die in the cradle where it lay, to misquote the bard. It was nurtured with shared participation and was then made to ring a joyous peal.

Tell me where is fancy bred,
Or in the heart or in the head?
Where begot, how nourished?
Reply, Reply.

It is engender'd in the eyes,
With gazing fed; and fancy dies
In the cradle where it lies.
Let us all ring fancy's knell;
I'll begin it, Ding, dong, bell.

William Shakespeare, *The Merchant of Venice*,
Act 3, Scene 2

Bibliography

Applebee, A. (1978) *The Child's Concept of Story*, Chicago: The University of Chicago Press.

Ashton Warner, S. (1980) *Teacher*, London: Virago.

Bandura, A. (1977) *Social Learning Theory*. Englewood Cliffs, NJ: Prentice-Hall.

Bennett, A. (1994) *Writing Home*, London: Faber.

Bettelheim, B. (1976) *The Uses of Enchantment*, London: Thames & Hudson.

Bradley, L. and Bryant, P. (1980) 'Why children sometimes write what they cannot read', in Frith, U. (ed.) *Cognitive Processes in Spelling*, London: Academic Press.

Bradley, L. and Bryant, P. (1985) *Children's Reading Problems*, Oxford: Blackwell.

Browne, A. (1986) *The Piggybook*, London: Julia McRae Books.

Bruner, J. (1966) *Towards a Theory of Instruction*, Cambridge, MA: Harvard University Press.

Chukovsky, K. (1963) *From Two to Five*, Berkeley: University of California Press.

Clark, M. (1976) *Young Fluent Readers*, London: Heinemann.

Clay, M. (1973) *What Did I Write?* Auckland: Heinemann.

Cowley, J. (1983) *Hairy Bear*, Auckland: Shortland Publications Ltd.

Cripps, C. and Cox, R. (1989) *Joining the ABC*, London: IDA.

Dodd, L. (1988) *Wake Up Bear*, London: Picture Puffins.

Donaldson, M. (1978) *Children's Minds*, London: Fontana Press.

Egan, K. (1988a) *Primary Understanding*, London: Routledge.

Egan, K. (1988b) *Teaching as Storytelling: An Alternative Approach to Teaching and Storytelling*, London: Routledge.

Egan, K. (1992) *Imagination in Teaching and Learning*, London: Routledge.

Eggleton, J. (1987) *Rat-a-Tat-Tat*, Auckland: Shortland Publications Ltd.

Freud, S. (1959) 'Creative writer and daydreaming', in *The Standard Edition of the Complete Psychological Works of Sigmund Freud*, Strachey, J. (ed.), London: Hogarth.

Frith, U. (1986) *Cognitive Processes in Spelling*, London: Academic Press.

Goswami, U. and Bryant, P. (1990) *Phonological Skills and Learning to Read*, Hove: Lawrence Erlbaum Associates.

Graves, D. (1983) *Writing: Teachers and Children at Work*, Exeter, NH: Heinemann.

Hall, E., Hall, C. and Leach, A. (1990) *Scripted Fantasy in the Classroom*, London: Routledge.

Holdaway, D. (1979) *The Foundations of Literacy*, London: Ashton Scholastic.

Jones, R. (1969) *Fantasy and Feeling in Education*, New York: New York University Press.

Labov, W. (1969) 'The logic of non-standard English', *Georgetown Monographs on Language and Linguistics*, 22, Washington, DC: Georgetown University Press.

Lewin, K. (1935) *A Dynamic Theory of Personality*, New York: McGraw-Hill.

Luria, A. *The Nature of Human Conflict*, New York: Liveright.

Maris, R. (1986) *'Are You There, Bear?'* London: Picture Puffins.

Meek, M. (1982) *Learning to Read*, London: The Bodley Head.

Meek, M. (1988) *How Texts Teach What Readers Learn*, Stroud: Thimble Press.

Meek, M. (1991) *On Being Literate*, London: The Bodley Head.

Opie, I. and Opie, P. (1969) *Children's Games in Street and Playground*, Oxford: Oxford University Press.

Ousby, J. (1992) 'Reading and the imagination', in Harrison, C. and Coles, M. (eds) *The Reading for Real Handbook*, London: Routledge.

Peters, M. (1985) *Spelling Caught or Taught*, London: Routledge & Kegan Paul.

Piaget, J. (1932) *The Language and Thought of the Child*, New York: Harcourt.

Read, C. (1986) *Children's Creative Spelling*, London: Routledge & Kegan Paul.

Rosen, M. and Oxenbury, H. (1989) *We're Going On a Bear Hunt*, London: Walker Books.

Schubert, I. and Schubert, D. (1987) *Little Big Feet*, London: Beaver Books.

Sendak, M. (1963) *Where The Wild Things Are*, London: Harper & Row.

Singer, J. (1973) *The Child's World of Make Believe: Experimental Studies of Imaginative Play*, New York: Academia Press.

Smith, F. (1978) *Reading*, Cambridge: Cambridge University Press.

Spreadbury, J. (1993) 'Family literacy in Australia', in Wray, D. (ed.) *Text and Context*, Widnes: UK Reading Association.

Stanovich, K. (1986) 'Matthew effects in reading: some consequences of individual differences in the acquisition of literacy,' *Reading Research Quarterly* XXI/4.

Sutton-Smith, B. (1988) 'In search of imagination', in Egan, K. and Nadander, D. (eds) *Imagination and Education*, New York: Teachers College Press.

Venezky, R. (1980) 'From Webster to Rice to Roosevelt', in Frith, U. (ed.) *Cognitive Processes in Spelling*, London: Academic Press.

Vygotsky, L. (1978) *Mind in Society*, Cambridge, MA: Harvard University Press.

Waddell, M. (1988) *'Can't You Sleep Little Bear?'* London: Walker Books.

Walkerdine, V. (1982) 'From context to text: a psychological approach to abstract thought', in Beveridge, M. (ed.) *Children Thinking Through Language*, London: Edward Arnold.

Waterland, E. (1985) *Read With Me: An Apprenticeship Approach to Reading*, Stroud: Thimble Press.

Werner, H. (1948) *Comparative Psychology of Mental Development*, New York: International Universities Press Inc.

Index

Opies, playground centred
  research 35
Ousby, Jack, reading and the
  imagination 41
overprotection, lack of fantasy
  skills development 38–9
ownership: Bear's birthday party
  17; direction of learning 22; and
  Little Witch's trips home 27–8

paper for writing 10–11
parental involvement 88–9,
  125–6; the Bear year 12, 16–17,
  22–3; Little Witch year 28–9,
  30–1, 121
Peters, Margaret, theories on
  spelling 62
phonemic knowledge and
  awareness 9–10, 44–6
physical contact and
  communication 96–7
planning and teacher autonomy
  128–9
playground centred research
  project, Opies 35
playgrounds 128
praise, importance of 92–3
pre-school 'incidental' literacy
  learning 45, 67
Primary Understanding, Egan
  41–2
problem solving, mathematics,
  Bear's birthday party 40, 100–1
problems at home, children with
  94; bereavement 14, 76, 95–6;
  family breakup 96–7
progress, children's awareness of
  own 54, 55, 61–2
proximal development, zones of
  55–6
punctuation, writing skills 47

rainbows, studying light 20,
  105–6

Rat-a-Tat-Tat, Jill Eggleton 45
Read, theories on spelling 62
reading 66–81; apprenticeship
  approach to 78; the Bear year
  8–9, 37–8, 75, 111; children
  needing help 76–7; delayed
  commencement 68, 69–72, 89;
  experience of learning to read
  66; family reading patterns
  69–72, 89; imaginative play and
  repeated practice 37–8;
  knowing text by heart and
  73–4; need for developed
  imagination 74–5; older child's
  breakthrough 93–4; particular
  favourites 74–5; pre-school
  incidental literacy 45, 67;
  remedial help for slow starters
  77; selecting books 79; sharing
  and interacting 72–4; slipping
  into 81; talking about reading
  process 75–6; teaching Bear
  8–9, 37–8, 75; writing in
  learning skills for 44
reading books, graded 67–8
reading with children 79–80
reading progression, short stories
  to long narratives 38
reading stamina, developing 38,
  79
reality and fantasy 36, 114;
  interweaving 65, 74; in play 35
relationship with mothers and
  teachers, imaginative play 39
remedial help, slow starters,
  reading 77
research: Bear facts 80–1; Bear's
  birthday party 99–101;
  development of study skills
  80–1; memories of Bear year
  112; school toilets 12–13
rhymes: phonemic awareness
  9–10, 45; waking the Bear
  18–19